# SOUTH AFRICA:
# A SKUNK AMONG NATIONS

# SOUTH AFRICA:

## A SKUNK AMONG NATIONS

## Les de Villiers

*The Author*

Les de Villiers is South African born. He obtained a
Masters degree in Linguistics before entering journalism
and eventually joined government service. Spending
five years in Canada as a diplomat and another five in
the United States where he headed South Africa's Information Services, he is a frequent public speaker and
often appears in television debates about his country.
He has written several novels.

14 Gloucester Road, London SW7

Published in Great Britain by Universal-Tandem
Publishing Co. Ltd, 1975

099301

Printed in Great Britain by The Anchor Press Ltd
and bound by Wm Brendon & Son Ltd
both of Tiptree, Essex

ISBN 4 2615974 8

# Contents

# List of Illustrations

*between pages 98 and 99*

# Introduction

In 1960 the Cape Town Afrikaans daily, *Die Burger*, took stock of South Africa's position on the world's popularity charts. In a blunt and honest appraisal this newspaper depicted South Africa as 'the skunk of the world'. Such, it concluded, was the lowly status that this country had to endure abroad. Fourteen years later this description—despite some signs of improvement—is still valid.

In an article published and syndicated by the *New York Times* in August 1971, I questioned the sincerity and methods of some of the men and institutions who helped to ruin South Africa's reputation abroad. This piece was headed 'A Scarecrow Image', because that is what South Africa's detractors have made of her in post-war years—a nightmarish thing which scares and infuriates peoples and nations to the end of the earth. 'The scarecrow image must persist at all costs', I concluded. 'After all, what excitement and incitement value could the real image have? It would simply make South Africa one of a crowd in our all too imperfect world society.'

This article struck a few responsive chords. There were strident ones too among the letters I received, but most of my correspondents were sympathetic. Many asked me to elaborate further. One, an American professor, suggested: 'Why don't you write a book to expose the world's dishonesty and double-standards in dealing with South Africa?' He hastily added: 'I personally hold no brief for South Africa's apartheid. But then I despise mass killings and suppression of peoples in Russia, Burundi, Uganda, Nigeria, Red China and a host of other civilized and semi-

9

civilized countries even more. What right does the world have to argue about technicalities in South Africa, while the real victims pile up elsewhere?'

The volume is an atempt at such an *expose*. It is neither a complete inventory of all the machinations to which South Africa has been subjected in the past three decades, nor an academic treatise on the psychology of modern propaganda warfare. It is simply a brief look at the various layers in the mask behind which its detractors have hidden the real South Africa. In peeling away at this mask I have found one element that permeates all the layers : double-standards.

In the past thirty years double-standard treatment and selective indignation has characterized most of the pronouncements and actions against South Africa in the world at large. There is one standard for South Africa, another for the rest of the world; one morality condemning real and imaginary wrong-doings in South Africa, another which tolerates gross sins elsewhere. This system of double-standards enables the Soviet Ambassador to attack South Africa at the United Nations as a 'slave society', while representing a country where Solzhenitsyn found an endless series of concentration camps and Robert Conquest counted some twenty million people exterminated since Stalin came to power.[1] Yet the Soviet representative castigates South Africa with impunity. In fact he earns thundering applause in the UN General Assembly.

But the practice of double-standards is not limited to the United Nations or to world politics. It threads through every international activity. Sport. Aviation. Art. Religion. Tourism ...

I was in London in July 1974 when Britain's Race Relations Board instructed travel agents to destroy or return copies of a brochure produced by the South African Tourist Corporation. Prodded by the Anti-Apartheid Movement the Board found that this travel publication contravened Britain's Race Relations Act by distinguishing between White and Black in its description of visa requirements for visitors to South Africa.

On this particular day when the news broke about the banning of SATOUR's booklet I happened to be visiting the offices of a London travel agent. As he tried to shake loose from a long-

1. Alexander Solzhenitsyn: *The Gulag Archipelago*. Robert Conquest: *The Great Terror*.

winded telephonic customer, I paged through the agent's dog-eared copy of *TIM*. Published by the International Air Travel Association *TIM* or the *Travel Information Manual* happens to be required reading for every conscientious agent. As I scanned this December 1973 edition I discovered to my surprise that it contained more 'objectionable' data on visas than any of the ten latest brochures produced by the South African Tourist Corporation.

In Australia, according to this manual, visas were not required from nationals of most Commonwealth countries—*provided* they were of 'wholly European origin'. The same provision was spelt out for New Zealand. Guatemala exempted most prospective visitors from obtaining visas in advance. Exceptions? 'Persons belonging to the black or yellow races'. These are some of the distinctions spelt out in *TIM* on behalf of IATA's membership. Incidentally, I believe this publication is still very much in use at most of Britain's travel agencies, but the Anti-Apartheid Movement and the Race Relations Board have yet to complain about it.

The world press has proved equally adept at double-dealing when it comes to South Africa. Having, for instance, devoted banner headlines and front-page treatment to a single shooting incident at Sharpeville in 1960 where sixty-nine people perished, most journals could scarcely find room to mention mass killings in the Sudan and other parts of Africa. While denouncing apartheid, which means self-determination for blacks in South Africa, as an 'anachronism', 'ill-advised', 'abhorrent' and so on, newspapers in America and Australia gladly praise efforts in their own countries to preserve and promote self-pride and self-help among Red Indians and Aborigines.

Political extortion, blackmail and bribery. These are elements which often feature in the vendetta against South Africa. In 1970 British Prime Minister Harold Wilson at first refrained from interfering with the forthcoming South African cricket tour. He was, however, eventually brought to heel when Black Africa's Supreme Council for Sport threatened to boycott the Edinburgh Commonwealth Games if the South African cricketers were allowed to visit Britain. 'We respect the man who starts to walk to the pavilion without waiting for the umpire's finger,' mused Mr Wilson when he explained his about-face on TV afterwards. But he wasn't talking about cricket. He was talking about extortion.

Ballot blackmail has been a regular feature of the world's dealings with South Africa ever since Black Africa became the United Nations' strongest voting bloc. Usually supported by Asian and Communist states in their tirades against South Africa, these Black nations often succeed in silencing the few remaining voices of reason with threats of voting reprisals. In 1974 a proposal to terminate South Africa's UN membership—introduced by Kenya, Mauritania and Cameroon—was debated at length while the Western 'Big Three' were apparently fumbling around for an excuse to use their veto power without incurring the wrath of Black Africa. Australia—a non-permanent member —informed the Council in advance that it would vote for South Africa's expulsion. A case of handing over the ransom even before any hostages were taken.

Strong-arm tactics and blatant bribery are not confined to South Africa's detractors in Africa. The Communist world had been in this game long before the independent African states increased in number to forty plus. In July 1974 South Africa was expelled from the World Gymnastic Championships at the congress of the International Gymnastics Federation (FIG) in Montreux, Switzerland. The motion to boot South Africa out was carried against all expectations by a narrow margin of two votes. Exclaimed the Vice-President of the South African Amateur Gymnastics Union, Ron Froelich, in anger : 'The Russian chief delegate came into the hotel bar and quite blatantly lifted the telephone to Moscow to get his orders on how to buy up the votes !'

As can happen when emotionalism takes over and reason and logic melt away in the heat of an argument, this effort of the world to extirpate South Africa sometimes borders on the absurd. In 1973, for example, London clergyman Paul Oestreicher found cause to assail South Africa for publishing a postage stamp depicting two cats in close proximity—one yellow and the other black. This feline pair marked the centenary of South Africa's Society for the Prevention of Cruelty to Animals. Contended Oestreicher : 'It would be illegal for white and black humans in South Africa to come that near to each other !' Added the daily *Australian* : 'Perhaps it should also be noted that while the two cats may be in close proximity the white one is well in the ascendant.'

On another equally absurd occasion British wit came to the rescue. In December 1973 the British magazine, *Race Today*, accused British Airways of misleading advertising. This airline, it was pointed out, used a seductive picture of a beautiful black girl to publicize its flights to South Africa. Contended *Race Today*: 'Any white man following up this promise of unbounded sexuality would be prosecuted under the Immorality Act in South Africa.' Retorted a spokesman for British Airways: 'Our poster for East Africa shows an elephant, but we're not suggesting . . . '

Addressing the UN Security Council during October 1974, South African Ambassador 'Pik' Botha pointed out that his government was as concerned about human rights, human freedoms and human dignity as any other in the world. 'Discrimination based solely on the colour of a man's skin cannot be defended,' he said. There were reprehensible incidents in South Africa, he conceded, but these were far outnumbered by positive examples of goodwill between races in his country.

For failing to accomplish perfection—something which has so far eluded the rest of the world as well—South Africa is pictured abroad as the worst miscreant of them all. A nation fit only to be tried, convicted and executed in public. The case against her is a loaded one, built on the understanding that while elsewhere the exception may prove the rule, in South Africa the exception *is* the rule. Those reprehensible incidents mentioned by the South African Ambassador in the Security Council are blown up out of all proportion and supplemented quite often with purely imaginary supporting 'evidence' to make the scarecrow image fit.

This is not a book about apartheid or separate development— South Africa's policy of separate freedoms and self-determination for the many Black nations, and the single White nation, within its present geographical borders. It is not the case for South Africa or a defence of her actions. More eloquent men than I have failed miserably to make themselves heard above the cacophony of South Africa's detractors. This is simply a brief, informal study of how one country happened to become a skunk among nations.

LES DE VILLIERS

*Pretoria*
*October 1974*

# I

# Abuse the Plaintiff

Cicero once said: 'When you have no basis for an argument, abuse the plaintiff.' Judging from the actions of the United Nations against South Africa over the past twenty-eight years there must be among its member states serious students of Cicero.

In 1963 UN press correspondent Thomas Franck had 'one sure answer' about what he would least like to be—a South African delegate at the United Nations. 'If the South Africa delegation spoke only Kiswahili, suffered collectively from a highly contagious version of Bright's disease and looked like the cast of a Frankenstein movie or a Charles Addams cartoon, they would not be more shunned and ostracized in the social and political world of the United Nations,' said Franck.

Some may contend that Mr Franck exaggerated; few, if any, will dare contradict him. South Africa's image and cause have turned sour at the so-called 'parliament of nations' almost from the very start. The roots of the poisonous growth which strangled South African membership in various UN agencies and threatens to do the same in the world body itself are firmly embedded in the charred soil of the immediate post-war era.

At the closing stages of the Second World War Field Marshal Smuts represented South Africa at the San Francisco Conference which led to the establishment of the United Nations. The South African Prime Minister worked incessantly. Apart from drafting the now famous preamble to the UN Charter, he served as Chairman of the Commission on the General Assembly. He was also responsible for amendments in connection with the Security and Social and Economic Councils.

Smuts was looked upon by all present as a great repository of wisdom and experience of peace and war. The Canadian Prime Minister at the time, Mr MacKenzie King, bestowed on Smuts, during his visit to Ottawa after the conclusion of the San Francisco deliberations, the title 'Counsellor of the Nation'. In the British House of Commons, Prime Minister Attlee paid Smuts this tribute : 'That preamble we owe largely to Field Marshal Smuts. His authoritative contributions to discussions at San Francisco were the result of that union of lofty ideals and practical wisdom that we have come to expect from him.'

These were happy days for Smuts. In South Africa he refused to pay any attention to sneering remarks by critics who labelled the San Francisco conference 'San Fiasco'. With certain reserva- tions the leader of the Opposition, Dr Daniel Malan, eventually also supported the ratification of South Africa's membership of the United Nations.

Smuts led the South African delegation to the first session of the United Nations General Assembly in 1946. Very much to his own surprise, India insisted that the position of the Indians in South Africa—a purely domestic affair—be discussed; India, the very country which has often insisted that she would not put up with any interference in *her* 'domestic affairs' even if these in- volved 'the end of Pakistan, the end of India, and the end of the world.' The South African Prime Minister pointed out that Article 2, paragraph 7, of the Charter stated clearly that nothing contained in the UN Charter shall authorize the world body to intervene in matters which were essentially within the jurisdiction of any member state. South Africa's problems, he maintained, were essentially within the jurisdiction of his own government. His words had little effect, least of all on the Indian delegation. The Indian motion was accepted.

On his return to South Africa, Smuts complained that he found himself up against a stone wall of prejudice at the very organization which he had so ardently helped to mould. A disillusioned and disappointed man, the South African Prime Minister told his Senate that 'unless nations are acknowledged as being sovereign and conduct their own internal affairs accord- ing to their own concept and their own system', there will be chaos in the world. 'People think that slavery still continues in South Africa,' he said. 'They think that we exploit people here.

This is the impression certain Communists and many others—and many of them are South Africans—continue to propagate and spread and, unfortunately, it is very difficult for us, and very expensive to fight such a campaign. An entirely new wind blows in the world today. A change is coming over the world and we feel the shock thereof! But we will hold our own.'

Two years later Smuts and his United Party were defeated at the polls. On 4 June 1948 Dr Daniel Malan, leader of the victorious National Party, took over the reins. 'In regard to our membership of the United Nations Organization,' said Malan, 'we wish to make it very clear that we, together with our predecessors in government, accepted it on the unequivocal understanding that there was to be neither external interference in our domestic affairs, nor any tampering with our autonomous rights. On this foundation we shall continue to build, and we shall steadfastly refuse to allow any country or power or organization to guide our destinies—that will be our duty.'

In this spirit the first delegation of the new National government proceeded to the third session of the United Nations General Assembly at Lake Success. As had happened under Smuts, their protest against interference in South Africa's domestic affairs fell on deaf ears. 'Apartheid', a word first coined by Malan in the 1948 election to describe South Africa's traditional race policy, has featured regularly on UN agendas ever since.

At the first session of the United Nations, Smuts faced an Assembly of fifty-one member states. Apart from South Africa, there were only three other African delegations present—Ethiopia, Liberia and Egypt. Excluding South Africa, there are today forty-one African nations accredited to UN headquarters at New York's Turtle Bay. Thirty-three of these have been seated since the beginning of 1960 and today they command, together with the Asian member states, an instant two-thirds majority in the General Assembly. The Third World Bloc—or as American Secretary of State Kissinger termed it, the alignment of the non-aligned—dominates the United Nations.

The Africans run the General Assembly almost by themselves and, elsewhere in the UN, willing allies from the Communist camp, as well as ballot-buyers from the West, usually help them to get what they want. Far-out moves by the African member states are often only deflected at the last moment by an American, French or British veto in the Security Council. And sometimes even these nations fail to stop the mob. As early as December 1964 UN press correspondent Aaron Einfrank reported as follows on the state of affairs in the organization's match-box-shaped New York headquarters :

'Because the Assembly usually acts according to the dictum that "what's White is wrong and what's Black is right", the Africans merely have to open their mouths with a loud tribal howl and an automatic two-thirds majority occurs, thanks to support from the Asian bloc and the Communists as well as from a smattering of pro-African states.'

Utilizing this 'automatic two-thirds majority' the African states have rammed through dozens of condemnatory resolutions on apartheid during the past twenty-eight years. An arms embargo was endorsed by the Security Council. South Africa's voice has been silenced step by step in virtually all the major non-political specialized agencies of the United Nations, ranging from the United Nations Food and Agriculture Organization to the World Health Organization. In 1974 she was even barred from participating in the UN General Assembly itself.

In 1965 the United Nations Economic Commission for Africa convened in Nairobi to find a cure for the many economic ailments of Africa's new Black nations—to get some meat on the bare *uhuru* bone left by the hasty retreat of the European colonial powers. International observers noted that South Africa, 'the best-qualified physician on African economic and technical ailments', was barred from attending.

The year 1974 found Black Africa, at a UN-sponsored world population conference, more intent on South Africa-baiting than problem solving. The problem at hand was very much that of newly independent Africa, where the population growth reached new record highs while food-production levels remained unchanged for years and even slipped in many cases. Suggestions from some Western experts that birth control be seriously considered were greeted with scorn and abuse by incensed Black delegates. Accusing these well-meaning experts of imperialism and racism, they suggested that the 'problem' of South Africa and apartheid should be tackled first.

Also in 1974 Dutch Overseas Development Minister Pronk

safaried in Tanzania. Meeting with President Julius Nyerere in Dar-es-Salaam, Jan Pronk was told that Tanzania could never make headway with White South Africa around to stunt its growth. The Dutch Minister proved his good faith and bland acceptance of this strange piece of logic by promising more Dutch gulden for the terrorist movement in southern Africa, channelling funds into destructive avenues instead of helping to build and develop Tanzania itself.

In the mid-sixties it was rumoured in Montreal that the African states were contemplating South Africa's expulsion from the International Civil Aviation Organization. To a Western world as yet not quite used to Black African logic, this seemed unthinkable. 'If the African states go ahead, they will prove just one thing: that racial animosity is more important to them than the problems of aviation they were convened to discuss', wrote the *Montreal Star*. The African states went ahead and were only narrowly defeated. This did not prevent them from trying, often successfully, to black-ball South Africa at a number of other supposedly apolitical world gatherings, including seminars on pollution and sea-bed utilization.

South Africa is still seated at the United Nations itself. But barely so. At the same 1970 General Assembly session where Red China's proposed admission gained majority support on the basis that the UN should be representative of all the world's nations—both sinners and saints—South Africa's credentials were questioned for the first time. The Credentials Committee eventually decided that South Africa's status as a member was in order, but the Assembly refused to endorse this view. As a compromise it was ruled that South Africa should remain seated for the time being.

In 1971 Red China was welcomed into both the Assembly and the Security Council, at the expense of Nationalist China, by a vote of 71 to 35 with 17 abstentions. While this mainland Chinese colossus entered the Turtle Bay complex with an estimated twenty-five million killed in its rulers' quest for absolute power, South Africa once again found herself fighting the waves of expulsion. And in 1972 Red China participated in the ouster game against South Africa charging that she did not 'deserve' to be a member. Once again the expulsion move failed narrowly.

There are some cynics who maintain that it's all a game—

that Black Africa does not really want to kill off South Africa's membership of the United Nations. After all, where would they find another whipping boy to distract attention from their own shortcomings? One expert even suggested that if South Africa did not exist it would have been necessary to invent her for the sake of the United Nations. How else could the world bypass road blocks like Ireland, Vietnam, Nigeria and a host of other real problems than by focusing attention on South Africa's 'crimes' ?

Arriving in New York in September 1973 for the twenty-eighth session of the UN General Assembly, South Africa's delegation already knew at the pencil-sharpening stage what would happen. There would be a credentials hassle and a mass walk-out of African representatives and their allies when South Africa's Foreign Minister mounted the podium to address the Assembly. And there would be the usual resolutions, rulings and documentation against apartheid—declared a punishable crime at the insistence of the Third World and the Communist camp.

It had become customary for African members to take a stroll whenever the South African viewpoint was aired. This, as a manifestation of their intolerance for viewpoints differing from their own, was a somewhat milder version of the treatment they gave Eric Louw—then South Africa's Foreign Minister—in 1961. At that session Louw dared to present a factual comparison between conditions for the Black man in South Africa and in other African states. This was done in reply to charges that the Black man in South Africa leads a subhuman existence. Mr Louw gave proof that the Black people of South Africa had a higher income *per capita*, better educational opportunities, far superior medical and social services and altogether a much higher standard of living, than any of the inhabitants of the newly independent African states. A motion of censure—the first of its kind—was engineered by Black Africa and adopted by the Assembly. His speech was struck from the record.

The *Washington Post*, a regular South African critic, noted : 'Nothing that South Africa has done and nothing that its representatives said, justified the mob-like censure which the United Nations visited upon that country and its Foreign Minister, Mr Eric Louw.'

It is doubtful that admonishments like these deterred Black Africa from introducing further censure moves. It was simply that stomping out of the Assembly in full view of the world whenever a South African spokesman dared to rise was more dramatic and satisfying than censuring; and it was a practice finely attuned to the demonstrative nature of the races of Africa. So South Africa's Foreign Minister and his advisers did not need a crystal ball in 1973 to predict a walk-out or to anticipate another credentials game. As for anti-apartheid resolutions there were almost a hundred precedents on record.

Developments went according to the regular script until the Ambassador from Mauritius rose in the Assembly on a point of order. Radha Kirshna Ramphul is a flamboyant man and he thoroughly enjoyed the task thrust upon his rounded shoulders as October chairman of the African group in the United Nations. South Africa, he argued in a vigorous high-pitched voice, could not be heard in the Assembly until her credentials were approved. Suddenly South Africa was faced with a new situation—one that could hardly be dismissed as only another toothless snap at her heels. In Pretoria Prime Minister Vorster announced that South Africa would not hesitate to withdraw from the world body if it became impossible for her to participate fully like any other member and to do so with decorum and honour.

In the meantime Ramphul's move was followed by another— the rejection of South Africa's credentials by the General Assembly. In the past Presidents of the Assembly could justify South Africa's continued presence by pointing out that there was no definite ruling for or against her credentials. Now suddenly there was a definite rejection of the South African delegation's letters of credence in the Assembly itself. For a while her membership seemed at an end until the 1973 Assembly President ruled that this rejection did not unseat the South African delegation.

Until 1973 the fireworks display on South Africa's membership was limited to the General Assembly, with its President stamping out stray flames before they could do any real harm to the fabric of the UN. Then in 1974 a political pyromaniac, Mr Bouteflika of Algeria, took the Presidential chair. When South African Ambassador 'Pik' Botha mounted the rostrum to make a brief statement, President Bouteflika's moustache twitched in obvious disdain. He simply refused to recognize the physical presence of South Africa's thickset representative. Ambassador

Botha reacted to this self-induced myopia by explicitly refusing to congratulate Mr Bouteflika on his election as President.

In past years South Africa always managed with some difficulty to clear the first hurdle—the Credentials Committee—before getting to the second—the General Assembly. In 1974 she tripped over the very first gate. The Assembly was informed that the Credentials Committee rejected South Africa's right to be at the UN. Next act? The Assembly voted on a similar motion and decided by 98 votes to 23—14 abstaining—that South Africa was not fit for membership of the world organization. The Third World and its Communist backers easily carried the day against Western dissenters.

Introducing the motion to have South Africa expelled from the United Nations for her alleged denial of human rights was Uganda's Foreign Minister, Elizabeth Bagaya.[1] Representing a country and a dictator which have become synonymous with oppression and the indiscriminate execution of dissidents, Uganda's female Foreign Minister hardly batted an eyelid when listing South Africa's alleged crimes. Seated in the Assembly were the Indian representatives apparently blissfully unaware that Amin had expelled their race from Uganda. Also listening attentively were several Black representatives whose leaders had at times found it necessary to express embarrassment at the cruel excesses of the zealous, sometimes comical, black dictator, Idi Amin. And there were Western representatives who often referred with horror to Amin's practices.

Why, asked some concerned observers, did nobody have the guts to object to this macabre performance? Commented one South African daily, *Die Burger*: 'It's amazing that some members of the General Assembly did not burst out laughing as nobody considered it advisable to express their indignation.' The humour, irony—and tragedy—of the situation indeed escaped some, while others may have exclaimed privately: 'It only hurts when I laugh.'

1. Miss Bagaya's term of office as Ugandan Foreign Minister was a brief one. On 29 November 1974 the London *Times* reported that 'the strikingly attractive Miss Bagaya', who became Foreign Minister in February of that year, was dismissed by President Amin. He claimed that 'she made love to an unknown European in a toilet at Paris Airport.' *The Sunday Telegraph* of 20 January 1975 reported: 'The former Foreign Minister is expecting a child which Amin is said to have fathered.'

On 30 September the General Assembly rejected South Africa's credentials, and then asked the Security Council to support a move for expulsion. Eventually ten of the Council's fifteen members voted to terminate South Africa's membership. Only by applying their veto did the United States, France and Britain prevent this from happening.

The irony of this performance did not escape unnoticed. Eric Sevareid, one of the best-known commentators on the CBS network, observed that it was interesting to note some of the nations which had voted for South Africa's expulsion in the Security Council. 'Indonesia, for example, where some ten years ago many tens of thousands of racially Chinese were murdered in communal rioting. Several Black African nations where the dominant tribe has set upon weaker tribes and more tens of thousands—men, women and children—have been slaughtered . . . With a straight face Russia and China, operators of their own vast Gulag Archipelago, voted to expel South Africa.'

'This,' said Sevareid, 'was the first serious attempt since the UN was founded to expel a member country. Had it succeeded it would not have been the end. The so-called Third World countries, who used to object that the UN was an exclusive Big Power club, would have done their best to turn it into their own club. As a British delegate warned, Arab, Communist, and poor nations may very well club together to expel the State of Israel.'

Said the *Christian Science Monitor*: 'Hardly any nation—and certainly not the Soviet Union and China, who supported the expulsion—could measure up fully to the standards of the UN Charter. If such standards were strictly applied, the UN would fast be emptied of members.' The *Chicago Tribune* pointed out that 'nearly every one of South Africa's ten critics are themselves guilty of violating the principles of the UN declaration'.

But the General Assembly had the final word. Before the year was out it voted by 91 to 22, with 19 abstentions, to suspend South Africa from its deliberations. The *Washington Post* was one in a chorus of Western voices which considered this impetuous and spiteful action indefensible. It suggested that the United States suspend her participation in the General Assembly in protest. The *New York Times* described the gag on South Africa as 'illegal and dangerous'.

The Arabs supported South Africa's suspension in return for

Black African backing on the Palestine issue, and were not slow in collecting their end of the bargain. Barely days after the suspension vote against South Africa in the General Assembly, the Palestinian terrorist leader, Yassar Arafat, turned up at the United Nations. Reported the *Washington Post*: 'Arafat was welcomed by the Asians and Africans as a hero.' The Afro-Arab alliance voted to restrict Israel's freedom to speak; the Israeli delegate was limited to one brief statement.

Black African nations were definitely not delinquent in living up to their side of the *quid pro quo*. Said one Israeli: 'If the Arabs had proposed that the world were flat, a resolution to that effect would have been passed overwhelmingly.'

These were the developments that prompted the United States Chief Delegate, John Scali, to caution the UN General Assembly against 'the tyranny of the majority'. He pointed out that resolutions were often adopted by Assembly majorities that represented only a small fraction of the world's population. 'The minority which is so often offended may in fact be a practical majority in terms of its capacity to support and implement its decision.' As the Chief Representative of a country which paid 25 per cent of the UN's bills, Mr Scali spoke with some authority.

It was at this time also that a South African newspaper, *Die Beeld*, weighed the anti-South African votes at the UN in terms of budget contributions. While South Africa contributed 0.5 per cent of the world organization's total funds, the forty-two other African states together were responsible for only 0.02 per cent. South Africa ranked twenty-fifth in terms of payments to the UN and while these twenty-five countries accounted for 92.12 per cent of the budget, the remaining 7.88 per cent share represented 113 member states—mostly anti-South African. The ninety-one countries which voted for South Africa's suspension at the General Assembly in November 1974 represented only 28.28 per cent of the organization's budget.

In the UN General Assembly South Africa often found herself supported by a single vote—that of Portugal. In 1974 this support slipped away. Suddenly there was no one left to object to the double-standard treatment meted out to South Africa; no one but the victim. A leftist post-*coup* Portugal had capitulated to terrorist forces in war-torn Guinea Bissau and Mozambique only months before the Assembly convened in 1974.

Feverish discussions were already under way for yet another hand-over to Communist-supported Black 'freedom' forces in Angola, amid unrest and killings.

Portugal's Foreign Minister Mario Soares rose in the General Assembly to attack apartheid and South Africa, earning tumultuous applause from the Third World and its Communist allies. Once again the irony escaped Soares and his audience. His criticism was directed at a South African delegation including White, Coloured, Indian and Black delegates. The Black representative, Chief Minister Kaiser Matanzima, owed his presence at the UN to his elected position as majority leader of the Xhosa nation in South Africa. Destined under apartheid to lead his nation to full independence in 1976 and full membership of the UN, Matanzima and the South African Government had been involved in the peaceful transition of power for fifteen years. In the Portuguese African territories, on the other hand, it required bloody uprisings to bring about a hasty retreat by the Portuguese Government—leaving the destiny of these areas in the hands of the most violent among a non-elected minority.

Long-term peaceful transition to Black independence in South Africa, based on majority democratic rule, was cause for abuse and vituperation, while capitulation to force and violence in the Portuguese territories earned adulation. Gerald L'Ange of the *Johannesburg Star* described the scene in the General Assembly when Mario Soares made his historic *volte-face* statement : 'African and other delegates queued to shake Dr Soares' hand, holding up the Assembly's general debate for nearly half an hour in a dramatic demonstration of Portugal's new popularity in the UN.'

Some of those cynics who regarded Black Africa's expulsion moves as a parlour game are seriously revising their opinions in view of the 1973 and 1974 episodes. The Third World and its Communist supporters are indeed bent on pushing one of the UN's founder members out of its glass-panelled halls. In fact, they have already appointed a new delegation to take the present official one's place. By 84 votes to 3, the General Assembly's Special Political Committee passed an African sponsored resolution declaring two South African terrorist movements, the African National Congress and the Pan-African Congress, as the only and authentic representatives of that country.

South Africa's soft-spoken Foreign Minister, a Rhodes Scholar and graduate in classics, Dr Hilgard Muller, argued in 1972 with a half-empty Assembly in favour of promoting dialogue and eschewing violence. His government, he explained, was in constant dialogue with the elected Black leaders within South Africa, as well as some beyond its borders. 'The repudiation of dialogue leads to reliance upon uglier means of settling differences, none more ugly and abhorrent than terrorism,' he said. 'We must speak with one voice on this scourge, without equivocation, because terrorism, no matter where it may erupt or what its current guise, cannot shed its essential characteristics : it is beyond the pale of order, of law, of decency, of society and humanity. We cannot for selfish or regional reasons move to stamp it out in one form or one region, while encouraging it in another.'

The UN's answer to Muller's plea was a prompt invitation to the leaders of the terrorist ANC and PAC movements to join the club. (One observer had the temerity to suggest that equal treatment also required invitations to terrorist movements in Europe, Latin America, the United States and the Near and Far East.[2]) While their colleagues were busy killing defenceless civilians, both Black and White, on the borders of South Africa, these self-styled Black Castros unleashed a verbal assault on the 'barbarous' South African Government which, they claimed, enslaved and plundered the Black peoples.

The irony of the situation was hardly commented upon by those present at this gala performance. Orwellian Newspeak was not the invention of either the ANC or PAC. For many years before their appearance on the New York scene, others have practised flagrant Newspeak. Especially in attacks on South Africa and apartheid this device served a definite purpose. This allowed them to say, in effect, 'War is Peace', 'Freedom is Slavery' and 'Ignorance is Strength', without fear of contradiction.

At Addis Ababa the Organization for African Unity promised to destroy all the vestiges of White civilization in Africa. The rivers, Black Africa promised, would run red with the blood of

2. In 1974 a Soviet-inspired plan for setting up a Palestine Liberation Organization government-in-exile, and according it U.N. status, surfaced. Aimed at Israel, this device caused little surprise since Israel has recently been increasingly subjected to the same double-standard treatment as South Africa.

Whites and their children. A war fund was created to assist so-called 'liberation armies' directed to the south. The same African states then proceeded to the United Nations, complaining that South Africa constituted 'a threat to world peace'. This is authentic Newspeak, 1984-style. War is peace and peace becomes war. The aggressors of Addis Ababa are the victims, and South Africa, which has offered to sign a non-aggression pact with any African state, is declared the aggressor.

In the General Assembly in 1962 the Soviet Foreign Minister drew applause when he described South Africa as 'the veritable private domain of slave owners'. The fact that the statement came from an official of a country which has earned for itself an unmatched reputation throughout the world as the perpetrator of acts of repression and terrorization seems not to have struck the UN or its members as ironic. Mr Gromyko, speaking from a home base littered with prisons and labour camps and with an enslaved population exceeding eleven million at one time, went ahead with impunity accusing South Africa of imaginary mis-deeds. Slavery has become freedom, and freedom, slavery.

The Soviet Minister's accusation in 1962 happened to coin-cide with the completion of the Berlin Wall, and preceded by only a few months the granting of self-rule to the Xhosa of the Transkei, the most advanced of the Black nations within South Africa. In 1974 Russia could hardly wait to add her signature to a treaty aimed at the suppression and punishment of 'the inter-national crime of apartheid'. At the same time the Russian Nobel prize-winning author, Alexander Solzhenitsyn, was bounced out of the country for describing the string of concentration camps and labour colonies which stain the face of the Soviet Union.

'Would, for example, the South African Republic be able to hold a black leader imprisoned for four years and subject him to torture, as was the case with General Grogirenko? No, the world's storm of indignation would long ago have blown the roof off his prison.' These were the words of Solzhenitsyn in a letter to the United States begging her to set a higher price on détente. But Russia is not the only country which gets away with murder at home while heaping abuse on South Africa for imaginary or smaller wrongs.

The double-standard game has been practised at the United Nations right from the outset when India in 1946 tackled

Premier Jan Smuts on the 'plight' of the South African Indian. While India, Pakistan and Ceylon concerned themselves over the past twenty years with the 'miseries' of their brethren in South Africa, tens of thousands died of hunger, violence and in wars on their own doorsteps. A handful in South Africa took Smuts up on his offer to pay for their repatriation to India. This advance party immediately signalled their fellow South African Indians to stay where they were as conditions in the motherland were 'unbearable'.

Despite legislation to the contrary, 'untouchables' in India still occupy the lowly position which their name so aptly signifies. While more than a million Indian Tamils remain stateless in Ceylon and non-nationals in India, these countries preoccupy themselves at the United Nations with a few hundred thousand South African Indians who happen to enjoy a *per capita* income six times that of India. Attentively the world listens as these Asian nations bemoan the position of the 600,000 Indians in South Africa—men, women and children who voted unanimously against repatriation when it was offered to them. But the same world seems to be quite unconcerned about the sad fate of 900,000 refugees who fled across the borders to escape religious persecution in India and Pakistan during the sixties—or that of the 500,000 Indians thrown out of Burma, tens of thousands expelled from Uganda and thousands victimized in Kenya and Tanzania.

Still very much playing at double-standards, the United Nations Commission on Human Rights decided in March 1967 to establish a special unit to investigate allegations of cruelty against prisoners in South African gaols, while in Saudi Arabia, according to the Anti-Slavery Society's report to the United Nations, slaves were still sold. The Society estimated that King Feisal and wealthy members of his family held some thousands of slaves. The year 1974 found the UN Human Rights Commission still condemning South Africa, Rhodesia and the Portuguese territories while ignoring urgent problems elsewhere in the world.

Gerald L'Ange of the *Johannesburg Star* was there. The resolutions on Southern Africa, he said, were adopted by large majority votes and with hardly any contentious debate. 'But the commission was thrown into typical discord when it came to deal with specific complaints of "gross violations" of human rights in eight other countries. These included complaints of mass tribal killings in Burundi, detention of 55,000 political prisoners in Indonesia, torture of hundreds of dissidents in Brazil, suppression of political rights in Iran, forged marriages in Tanzania, interrogation by torture of thirty people detained by the British Army in Northern Ireland and discrimination against Indians in Guyana.'

The eight cases, L'Ange pointed out, had been selected from more than 7,000 by a panel which saw them as showing a 'consistent pattern of violation'. Reported L'Ange: 'A proposal that the eight cases be more closely investigated ran into stiff opposition, notably from the Soviet Union, which has good reason to fear that any such move might create a precedent for inquiry into its own shortcomings in the field of human rights.' All eight cases were shelved until 1975 and the Commission went on to Southern Africa, mustering the usual automatic vote— rather like a beginner in front of the piano who constantly shies away from more intricate and involved compositions and thankfully returns to basic finger practice, at which he finds himself quite adept.

Burundi, which rated brief mention for the mass killings there before her case was hastily shelved, sponsored an anti-South African resolution in the General Assembly—accusing the Pretoria regime of racism, cruelty and a few other misdeeds. The South African minority Government, it claimed, had no right to represent the people of that country. Meanwhile, the minority Tutsi tribe (barely 20 per cent of the population) were killing off the majority Hutu by thousands to stay in power in Burundi. Nobody is quite sure of the number killed in the past few years. Everybody agrees, however, that the body-count must be in tens of thousands.

Jeremy Greenland lived in Burundi and was an eyewitness to some of these killings. 'Throughout May and half of June 1972 the excavators were busy every night in Gitega and Bujumbura burying the dead in mass graves', he wrote. 'Those arrested were usually dead the same night, stripped and practically clubbed to death in covered lorries on the way to prison, then finished off there with clubs at nightfall. Using bullets would have been wasteful.' And the United Nations: 'The United Nations says little, even when its own vehicles are requisitioned and used to take Hutu to their death. It was ironic to see Land-Rovers marked UNICEF being used for this purpose', explained Greenland in the London *Times* during January 1974.

Unconcern also marks the UN's attitude to the Sudan killings, averaging 100,000 a year for several years. The Biafran war, too, was immediately declared out of bounds for the United Nations as it was 'an internal affair' for Nigeria to solve. Lasting thirty months, this war cost two million lives as a result of starvation and malnutrition apart from battle casualties—and forced five million Black souls into refugee camps. The UN chose to remain an observer. While all this was going on it devoted its undivided attention and energy to the really pressing problems of the world. South Africa, for instance.

This double-standard also manifests itself in the selective indignation displayed by the UN's chief executives. In 1964 Secretary-General U Thant tried to save the lives of two Black men who murdered one of their own race, a State witness. They were tried in South Africa, found guilty and sentenced to hanging. At the time the Africa correspondent of the *New York Times*, Lloyd Garrison, reported that 70,000 people had lost their lives in civil strife in Cameroon. This small matter went unnoticed. U Thant's successor, Kurt Waldheim, reacted immediately when he learnt about the death of eleven rioting Black miners at Carletonville. South Africa, Waldheim insisted, should admit his representative to the inquiry into the mine shooting. On the other hand he managed to ignore mass killings in Burundi and Sudan and several shootings in India. Even public executions in countries such as Nigeria, Zaïre and Guinea failed to stir U Thant or Waldheim into action.

In the early sixties the United Nations established a Special Committee on South-West Africa. In 1962 South Africa was accused of exterminating the native inhabitants and of militarizing this territory. South-West Africa, it was alleged, constituted a threat to world peace.

The Chairman and Vice-Chairman of the Committee were invited by South Africa to scrutinize her behaviour in this territory, which had been placed under South Africa's control by the old League of Nations. They accepted and were given the opportunity to see whatever they wished to see and to listen in private to a number of deputations.

On the basis of their on-the-spot observations the two gentlemen, Mr Vittorio Carpio and Dr S. Martinez de Alva, issued together with the South African Government a joint *communi-*

*qué* refuting the charges. Both were promptly replaced by others who had never been to South-West Africa—men who had not yet been weakened and confused by first-hand details. The *communiqué* was treated as if it did not exist; it was suppressed as a UN document.

Encouraged, no doubt, by their success at the United Nations, the African states in 1960 decided to take their dispute over South-West Africa to the International Court of Justice in The Hague. This territory, occupied by South Africa on behalf of the Allied powers during the First World War, was generally viewed as the Achilles heel of the White Government.

In 1920 South Africa agreed to administer South-West Africa under a compromise Mandate, which was recognized as being closely related to outright annexation. 'The mandatory,' it was stated, 'shall have full power of administration and legislation over the territory . . . as an integral part of the Union of South Africa, and may apply [its] laws.'

The Mandate from the League of Nations also stipulated that 'the mandatory shall promote to the utmost the material well-being and the social progress of the inhabitants of the territory'. It required freedom of conscience and religion, and prohibited the slave trade, trafficking in arms and liquor, fortifications or military bases.

In 1962, two years after Ethiopia and Liberia had filed their complaint against the South African administration on behalf of the African bloc, the World Court decided by the narrowest of margins—by 8 to 7 votes—that it had competence to hear the case. When they opened their case in the preliminary proceedings Ethiopia and Liberia listed extensive charges.

They contended that the Mandate was still legally in existence and that South Africa was obliged to report on her administration to the UN. Their factual case was founded on the allegation that South Africa acted in bad faith towards the inhabitants of South-West Africa by applying policies designed to oppress, suppress and exploit them. These charges covered a wide field of South Africa's administration of the territory. They alleged violations of the fundamental obligation conferred by the Mandate. Specific accusations were largely based on tales told at the United Nations by so-called 'petitioners'—self-styled political exiles from South-West Africa.

In refuting the case put up by Ethiopia and Liberia, South Africa took the point that if the Mandate still existed, it did not follow that she should be accountable to the United Nations. South Africa had an obligation to report to a specific organ of the League, namely, the Council. After the Second World War, however, the League was dissolved and with it the obligation. Moreover, the UN was not in any way a general successor in law to the League.

On the factual issue, South Africa countered with a written presentation of nearly 3,000 pages. Fifteen expert witnesses, out of a list of thirty-eight presented to the court, were called.

It was at this stage that Ernest A. Gross, New York international lawyer and sometime US delegate to the UN, who acted on behalf of the African states, ran into problems. He realized that it was not quite as easy to substantiate before a court of law charges which were accepted without scrutiny in the emotional atmosphere of the United Nations. Proof would be needed. At no stage in the case, however, did he show any sign of calling witnesses—least of all the South-West Africa 'petitioners'. Even an outright offer by South Africa to pay the expenses of these petitioners, in order to cross-examine them in the World Court, did not stir him into action.

His next move was dramatic and drastic. Gross abandoned all charges of oppression and based his case entirely on the contention that South Africa had acted contrary to a so-called norm or standard of non-discrimination or non-separation. This, he contended, was a norm or standard created by the overwhelming consensus of the international community.

With this about-face it became clear that Ethiopia and Liberia would have to accept all factual evidence put forward by South Africa. This they did. It meant also that the facts contained in the joint Carpio/De Alva *communiqué* were fully endorsed by those two countries, despite the Special Committee's refusal even to recognize its existence in 1962.

In reply to Gross's new case for Ethiopia and Liberia, South Africa once again countered with evidence by world-renowned experts. Fifty countries which by law and official practice differentiate between groups, classes or races were mentioned—forty of them members of the United Nations, including Ethiopia and Liberia themselves.

When Ethiopia and Liberia made this dramatic about-face in the International Court of Justice, realizing that far-fetched accusations at the United Nations did not enjoy the same automatic acceptance in a court of law, Counsel for South Africa noted: 'The abandonment of the charge of oppression and the admission of the true facts which so abundantly refute that charge had a very important practical effect on the respondents' position, because that had the effect of clearing South Africa's name of these charges, at least before the court and to a large extent before the whole world, if only the world would get to know about it.'

' . . . if only the world would get to know about it.' Barely three weeks after the conclusion of the case on 29 November 1965 the General Assembly of the UN once again passed a condemnatory resolution on South-West Africa. The charges? 'Oppression', 'militarization' and a 'threat to world peace'.

Spearheaded by the African and Asian members the General Assembly proved itself to be no less impervious to facts than the Special Committee on South-West Africa, which slammed its door in the faces of its own Chairman and Vice-Chairman when they dared speak the truth. 'In this world,' said Douglas Jerrold, 'truth can wait, she's used to it.'

The South-West Africa case was to cost South Africa well over a million dollars, while Ethiopia and Liberia and their African backers must have put up moneys well above this sum although these same states have experienced considerable difficulty in paying for their UN club membership at rates as low as 0.04 per cent of the total budget; which is not even enough to pay the keep of their missions in New York. Ethiopia's population averages an annual income *per capita* of some US $80.

Long before the World Court decided on the merits of the South-West Africa case, the Secretary-General of the Organization of African Unity promised its members a decision in their favour. The decision would go against South Africa, he predicted, and provide a brand-new weapon in the struggle against the 'white supremacists'. On 18 July 1966 the World Court in The Hague ruled that Ethiopia and Liberia had no standing in the matter before the court. In effect, this meant a decision in favour of South Africa.

The General Assembly then saw a feast of acrimony which

33

turned the stomachs of even the seasoned UN-watchers. The target was the World Court which had dared to come to the 'wrong' decision. The talking was done mostly by Black Africa, demanding that those men in robes at The Hague should do what they were expected to do, instead of delivering an impartial legal judgement based on the facts presented to them. The World Court, it was decided, should be changed drastically to ensure the 'right' decisions in future. In October 1966 the Assembly duly pronounced, by 114 votes to 2, that South Africa's Mandate in South West Africa had ceased. Seven months later it created 'a new administration' for the territory—The UN Council for South-West Africa.

At the end of 1968 the United Nations renamed the territory 'Namibia' and declared South Africa's presence 'illegal'. South African officialdom was given until 4 October 1969 to vacate their posts in 'Namibia'. Wry comment came from one South African observer, who remarked that the name for the territory which the UN claimed to administer was quite appropriate. After all, the Namib desert (from which 'Namibia' is derived) tends to conjure up trembling hallucinations on its sandy horizons. From South-West Africa, however, came complaints. The South-West African National Union—one of the militant minority parties which supported UN interference—complained that it had not been consulted. 'Our people should have been asked first before the christening ceremony was staged.'

The newly established Council for Namibia was not in the mood to be deterred by friend or foe from 'occupying', 'renaming' and 'ruling' its newly acquired charge in Africa. Gloating over pin-studded maps of 'Namibia', they were intent on going through all the motions which typify a full-fledged administration. They even issued George Houser, an activist member of the American Committee on Africa, with a 'visa' to 'Namibia'. Houser seems to have doubted its validity; he has certainly not yet attempted to present it to the real authorities at Windhoek airport. Then came the idea of issuing a special set of postage stamps for 'Namibia'. It is one that first appealed to the Council for Namibia, and eventually appalled them. Some members found it intolerable that both the territory and the name 'Namibia' were printed in white 'when the very thing they are fighting is White control of the territory'. For several days the stamps—six million in all—remained locked in safes in New York and Geneva. From South-West Africa came a suggestion—why not simply dip the whole supply in black ink?

The Western world was showing signs of embarrassment. What little remained of the UN's prestige was rapidly eroding under the burden of unrealistic resolutions, deadlines and demands set by the Afro-Asians on the matter of South-West Africa. On 4 October 1969 the South African authorities were still going about their business in the territory while Black Africa fumed with anger in the hallowed halls of the Turtle Bay complex. There was a proposal that the United Nations should 'force its way' into South-West Africa. Top United Nations officials and the Secretary-General of the Organization of African Unity, it was suggested, should hold a meeting in 'Namibia' during 1971; which was almost as ridiculous as considering the idea of a NATO meeting in Moscow. Yet the world organization mulled over this possibility for weeks on end.

Eventually it was decided to approach the World Court again. This time the Afro-Asian world—and the Communists—were assured of the 'right' decision. After all, in the years since 1966 they managed to pack the Court to an extent where the outcome on South African matters was beyond any shadow of doubt. The Security Council, instructed by the General Assembly, which in turn was manipulated by the Afro-Asian members, asked the International Court of Justice for an advisory opinion on the legal consequences for UN members of South Africa's continued presence in South-West Africa. In short, did South Africa have any legal rights in the territory? Back came the reply: South Africa had no rights in the territory.

The case itself—although lacking any element of surprise—was not without its interesting moments. The United Nations maintained that in its 'Namibia' all the peoples wanted independence as a whole, while South Africa insisted that in reality there were in South-West Africa various Black and Coloured 'nations', plus a White group, each preferring to order its own affairs.

The population picture of the territory—total inhabitants less than a million, area about equal to that of California—is best illustrated by a Bushman legend. According to this story it was Naua (or fate) who peopled the earth by throwing a lump of clay on the ground. The lump broke into many pieces, and the large pieces became the big tribes, and the small pieces the small tribes. Today 'Naua's broken pieces' lie strewn across South-West Africa, presenting a diversity of race and language with which few parts of the world can compare.

The rival arguments in favour of forced unity or of separate development were leading nowhere. So South Africa suggested that the peoples of South-West Africa be asked in a UN-controlled plebiscite to state their preference. At the same time the peoples of the territory could indicate whether they preferred South African or UN administration. The Court rejected this proposal, informing South Africa that it did not find itself in need of further arguments or information. Facts are of little importance when the conclusion is foregone.

The United Nations at last had the decision in hand which they had worked for all these years. But there was a snag: how could South Africa be evicted from 'Namibia'? Western and Latin American member states stepped in to prevent the UN from adopting another series of toothless resolutions. They initiated dialogue between the newly appointed UN Secretary-General, Kurt Waldheim, and the South African Government. For once it looked as if there might, after all, be a way out. Waldheim even accepted an invitation to visit South-West Africa and to be confused with first-hand facts—something that his predecessor, U Thant, had consistently refused to do.

The UN decided at last to talk to the real administrators of the territory instead of playing map games in a secluded East River office complex. But not for long. At the end of 1973 Black Africa had its way. The dialogue was ended by the United Nations. Announced Paul Lusaka, Zambian President of the Council for Namibia: 'The only way to end South African rule in South-West Africa is by armed struggle.'

When Secretary-General Kurt Waldheim dared to meet South Africa's Foreign Minister Muller for discussions in Geneva on the South-West Africa question without specific permission, he was censured by Black Africa. Vicious stories were circulated at the United Nations about Waldheim's alleged 'Nazi past' and 'suspect racial views'. The Black member states have a way of always getting what they want at the United Nations.

In a television interview African Ambassadors were asked why they devoted so much of their time and energy to the 'liberation' of South Africa, instead of trying to improve the miserable lot of their own impoverished and disease-ridden peoples. It is all very simple, came the reply, South Africa must be 'liberated' so that it could be 'possessed'. Once it became the 'possession' of Black Africa, it would provide all the riches needed to develop the other states.

Meanwhile, repeated offers by the South African Government to assist African states in their own development are, with rare exceptions, declined. Instead, these states have attempted to coerce the United Nations into applying an outright trade embargo against South Africa. The refusal of Western countries to sever their formidable trade relations with South Africa is strongly disapproved, but the African states themselves have failed to abide by their self-imposed trade ban. At an OAU meeting in March 1965, Kenya, Uganda, and Tanzania, among others, complained that 'while they were making themselves poor' through boycott of South African goods, some of the other African states, and Red China and East Germany, were continuing to trade with South Africa.

'Generally, the campaigning for a South African boycott is an amateur performance and on both sides of the Iron and Bamboo Curtains professionals are coolly ignoring the slogans, the UN speeches by the Soviet Ambassador, the Guinean Ambassador and others,' remarked Arnold Beichman of the *New York Herald Tribune*. Africa's imports from South Africa increased from $292,487 million in 1966 to $680,355 million in 1974.

In 1966 the African states once again assailed the Western countries for failing to act against South Africa in the United Nations. 'These states have repeatedly professed strong opposition to apartheid but the eloquence of their words has not been matched by their deeds,' it was charged. Western delegates have indeed been 'eloquent' enough in their verbal onslaught on South Africa to satisfy the gallery.

At times, however, they do not quite receive what they bargained for. One clear example was provided in December 1964, when the United States, often merciless in attacking South Africa, found herself on the receiving end. Charges against the United States and Belgium ranged from genocide to aggression, from imperialism to nefarious action, from massacre to cannibalism. Words like 'abhorrent', 'repugnant' and 'repulsive' spiced the verbal assault by Black Africa, which was outraged because the United States and Belgium had dared to save White hostages from Black rebels in the Congo.

'I have served in the United Nations from its inception off and on for seven years,' said US delegate Adlai Stevenson, 'but never before have I heard such irrational, irresponsible and repugnant language in these chambers . . .' In December 1964 *Time* magazine suddenly discovered that 'African civilization—with its elaborate trappings of a half a hundred sovereignties, governments and UN delegations—is largely a pretext'. The sane part of the world, decided *Time*, could only wonder whether Black Africa should be taken seriously at all, or whether, for the forseeable future, it was beyond the reach of reason.

Israel provides another example. Voting on South African issues with the Black states, assisting their development in numerous ways and even donating moneys for the OAU's terrorist drive against Southern Africa, Israel acquired for herself an envied status in emergent Africa. Then came the Yom Kippur war against the Arabs. Overnight all Black Africa severed relations with Israel. Her only real friends proved to be the United States, Portugal, the Netherlands and South Africa.

For Israel this was a rude awakening. Yosef Lapide, who writes for Tel Aviv's largest circulation daily, *Ma'Ariv*, felt the need to unburden himself in view of this ingratitude by Black Africa. 'Well, the so-called liberated African states are, with a few exceptions, a bad joke and an insult to human dignity', Lapide wrote. 'They are run by a bunch of corrupt rulers, some of whom, like Idi Amin of Uganda, are mad according to all the rules of psychiatry. I feel unburdened when I say this; I wanted to say this all these years, and all these years I had the feeling that we fool the public when, for reasons of diplomacy, we do not tell them that the majority of Black African states are one nauseating mess.'

Lapide found that 'the lowliest of Negroes in South Africa has more civil rights than the greatest Soviet author; the most oppressed Negro in South Africa has more to eat than millions of Africans in "liberated" countries'. And, he added, the 'most rabid White extremist in South Africa will not treat Negroes in the way Negroes treated—and still treat—Whites in the Congo, in Uganda and in other African states'. The people advocating 'progress', who were so worried about the rights of the majority in South Africa, Lapide added, have never raised their voices for the majority in Hungary or in Cuba, in Red China or in Egypt.

'In a half a dozen states—including Ethiopia—thousands of persons die every day of hunger, while the rulers travel by Cadillac and steal the food that is being sent to aid their subjects,' he remarked. 'Only in the sick minds of "progressives" do the babies die of starvation with a smile on their lips because the ruler who starves them to death has a black skin.'

'For the life of me,' he concluded, 'if I must choose between friendship with Black Africa, as it is today, and friendship with a White state that is orderly and successful, and contains a blossoming Jewish community, then I prefer South Africa. The only pity is that we waited until the Blacks threw us out.'

Such disillusionments do not always last. The Western nation which dares to engage in Lapide talk at the United Nations must beware. It can easily find itself running with the Southern African hares, hounds yapping at their heels, instead of being safely at the back of the canine pack. For every outburst like Lapide's there are tens of articles by Western apologists placating the Third World and its allies. On 4 February 1966, however, even the left-liberal magazine, *Life*, was unable to contain itself any longer. 'During the past two years, eight countries (in Africa) have undergone *coups*, some more than once, five in the last three months alone', *Life* stated. In one newly independent country tribal warfare resulted in the death of 40,000 men, women and children. In another 8,000 were killed in a revolt.

'No one would deny that membership in the United Nations has done a great deal to train African diplomats in the form— and sometimes the content—of parliamentary practice', said *Life*. 'There is something offensive, none the less, in hearing elegant pronouncements about the lack of human rights in South Africa from a delegate of a nation where a human right, if it started acting up in the street, would be incarcerated forthwith.'

Some time ago the Nordic countries, no doubt impressed by the 'elegant pronouncements', stepped to the front of this holy Black crusade against South Africa. They were suddenly no longer content merely to string along on the march to Pretoria. South Africa spotted an opportunity. She assumed that, as Western nations, the Nordic group would be more interested in facts than the African trouble-makers. This assumption proved extremely naive. An official invitation extended to the Foreign Ministers of the Nordic countries to visit South Africa as a group 'at a time convenient to them, with every facility to go where they pleased and to meet whomever they wished', was declined rather curtly. The African nations are obviously not the only ones who live in constant fear of facts concerning the South African situation.

Latin American countries dubbed the African nations in the United Nations the *Aplandora*—the steamroller. In the Assembly this steamroller dictates 'world opinion' and 'world conscience' on South African policies. In the Security Council it may eventually force a show-down.

In the opinion of many delegates, the African bloc is shifting the emphasis of the UN's work away from constructive attempts to maintain peace and towards pure propaganda for African interests. South Africa has always been very strongly in favour of a move 'back to San Francisco'. Only by following the original UN Charter, she contends, could the UN become a centre for harmonizing the actions of nations. She has protested often, and in no uncertain terms, against an ever-growing willingness by the African nations to violate the terms of the Charter. In this complaint, according to the *New York Times* in 1966, she is not alone. Many of the fifty-one founding members, feel that the Charter is being violated and that the rules and practices evolved during twenty years of experience are being swept aside.

The United Nations have in many ways simply become an extension of the Organization of African Unity, bent on destroying the White 'regimes' of Africa. Its various committees have been wedded and knitted and plaited together with a collection of anti-apartheid movements and terrorist organizations. In Oslo terrorist chieftains from Africa gathered in 1973 under UN auspices to plan strategy. A year later the Special Committee on apartheid went on an expensive junket to 'publicize its efforts' and to meet with anti-apartheid elements in churches, schools, universities and labour unions throughout Europe and Britain. At considerable expense to the already bankrupt UN, the whole Security Council was moved to Africa for a special session. The main theme : South Africa.

During the 1974 session West Germany applied for admission to the United Nations. She soon found out who ran the show.

Black Africa's blackmail tactics were thinly veiled. West Germany was told to toughen her approach to South Africa if she seriously wanted to be allowed in on the first vote. Chancellor Willy Brandt obliged in his maiden address in the General Assembly. He promised that the Federal Republic of Germany would 'support the United Nations resolutions aimed at liquidating the anachronistic remnants of colonialism', and that this applied 'not least to our neighbouring continent of Africa'.

Sometimes these Western powers find themselves exposed at home for dabbling in this dishonest practice of selective indignation to please Black Africa. The *Christchurch Press*, for one, in January 1974 found it a national shame that the New Zealand Government should try to make its policies towards its Pacific dependencies more acceptable by confirming the attitudes, some of them quite outrageous, of some of the least responsible members of the United Nations'. New Zealand's opposition to racial policies in Southern Africa, it said, expressed national concern. 'But New Zealand can take little credit for associating herself with some of the more extreme resolutions sponsored by the Africans.' In the long run, the *Christchurch Press* concluded, New Zealand will achieve more by making clear her abhorrence of prejudice and persecution in many parts of Africa and in other parts of the world, instead of concentrating only on South Africa.

Australian MP, R. V. Garland, who served as parliamentary adviser to his country's UN Mission during that same session, returned to Canberra disillusioned. 'The General Assembly and the Security Council have both now become places for votes to be cast for the impression they make rather than on the justice of the case', he wrote in the *Sydney Morning Herald* of 4 January 1974. 'There are interminable speeches, of doubtful relevance and factual content, almost all carefully sent home, and previously referred to "friends" for comment; here a passage slotted in to please one, there a diatribe condemning someone else.'

The British Ambassador to the United Nations, Sir Donald Maitland, was somewhat more specific. The General Assembly should seek practical solutions instead of indulging in 'exercises in fruitless rhetoric', he said. 'What good has been done by passing resolutions which have been disregarded'? The only value he saw in the numerous resolutions passed annually on South Africa was that they allowed 'frustrations to be sublimated'.

41

Referring to issues like South Africa and South-West Africa, Sir Donald said that the Assembly agenda was taking on a 'rather dog-eared quality' and some items featured so frequently that the agenda risked becoming 'a caricature of itself'. He concluded : 'This General Assembly has divorced itself from reality, from the real world outside.'

Despite its critics the UN will continue under its own momenttum. It will remain Alice in Slanderland as far as South Africa is concerned. A large portion of the paper-waste and word-pollution will be apportioned to South Africa by the real manipulators of Turtle Bay—the Third World and the Communist camp. In 1970 the UN was already spending 28 million dollars on churning out 773 million pages of documentation—enough to fill 260,000 books of average length, and so to stack a fair-sized library. During the same year there were 117 conferences and meetings held under UN auspices every day. In 1974 Secretary-General Waldheim proudly proposed setting up a round-the-clock 'freedom radio' in Zambia under UN auspices to tell the people of South-West Africa about the UN's efforts to liberate them.

Under the guise of acting on behalf of world opinion—or a world conscience—as personified by the so-called Parliament of Man in New York, the African states have set themselves the target of eliminating the existing order in South Africa. Within a world where, since World War II, more than 120 revolutions, wars and civil wars have caused widespread death and destruction, South Africa presents a tranquil picture. The pretext used for the attacks on this country is its policy of apartheid or separate development. Yet, the same treatment was meted out to the Portuguese territories and Rhodesia where racial policies were totally different from South Africa's. In Mozambique, for example, long before the terrorists take-over, assimilation—a few steps beyond integration—was the officially approved line of approach.

On 10 October 1973 even the *Johannesburg Star*, an antigovernment daily, had to concede that neither of the two opposition parties in South Africa appealed to the country's detractors in the United Nations. One of these two parties, the Progressive Party, stands for gradual integration, but 'the Special Committee on Apartheid rejected out of hand the race policies of the United and Progressive Parties as being a perpetuation of discrimination'. The homelands policy was described as a 'fraud', the *Star* observed. 'This attitude reflects a tacit support for subversion and revolutionary action and rejection of *all* peaceful solutions. Yet the UN's role should be to preserve peace as well as push for progress.' The London *Times* remarked: 'The African Communist objective is not limited to inducing the South African Government to repeal its laws; it is to bring on a full scale revolution.'

These are the stakes Africa and its Asian and Communist allies are playing for in the UN. The OAU seeks an end to all White vestiges in Africa and the rivers running red with White blood. Trailing along, and paying the piper, are several Western nations, fearful that non-co-operation may boomerang and expose them to similar attacks.

C. A. W. Manning, Professor Emeritus at the London School of Economics, points out that individuals have opinions, states do not. Countries or states simply have postures. These postures 'are a matter not of opinion but of policy'. Statesmen deliberate, weighing pros and cons, and the line they adopt is not necessarily a direct reflection of anyone's opinion in particular, Manning said. 'International politics are not a conversation. They are more in the nature of a game.' The UN game is played with loaded dice, heavily weighted against South Africa.

'We in South Africa must, therefore, be forgiven if we say that this kind of world conscience really does not impress us,' former South African Premier Verwoerd once declared. It was clear, he said, that in the field of international politics the attitude of the Western nations, to whom South Africa's destiny was linked, was not based on principle. For purely political and economic reasons, to further their own self-interest, the Western nations followed a line dictated by the numerically stronger Afro-Asians, combined with the Communists.

The African bloc rammed through an arms embargo against South Africa in 1964. It severed South African membership in various non-political specialized UN agencies. With its membership rights having been terminated, suspended or otherwise reduced over the past few years in nine specialized agencies, South Africa retains full rights only in the International Atomic Energy Agency and in the economic bodies affiliated with the UN —the World Bank, the International Monetary Fund and the general agreement on tariffs and trade (GATT). (South Africa's tenuous hold on its membership of the UN and its agencies slipped a little more with her suspension from the World

Meteorological Organization in 1975). Culmutatively the wild debates which usually accompany these moves to isolate South Africa diplomatically, economically and culturally also serve to promote a ludicrous picture of the victim.

Already in the fifties the *Natal Mercury* expressed its concern over 'the utterly absurd fabrications being disseminated through the UN Committee on Colonialism about "poison-gas factories" in the sands of South-West Africa and the establishment of a West German rocket base in the territory'. The 'poison-gas factories' turned out to be a mirage. The 'rocket base' did exist in the form of a rather small and not very significant weather station !

'South Africans may laugh at these absurdities', added the *Mercury*, 'but the trouble is that the thought processes of a world that is highly critical of this country's racial doctrines have been so cunningly indoctrinated that millions will believe this colourful nonsense.'

On his return from the first session of the United Nations some twenty years ago, Field Marshal Smuts complained that it was very difficult and very expensive for South Africa to fight the propaganda campaign launched against her by the UN. The *Sunday Express* sympathized. South Africa's efforts to solve her racial and political problems 'are gravely embarrassed by a formidable and increasing mass of ill-informed, adverse opinion abroad', said the *Express*.

'So far South Africans have not bothered their heads very much about opinion overseas beyond making little jokes about the ignorance of outsiders,' it added. 'But the time has come to consider whether this happy complacency should continue; for if things are allowed to drift, the view of this country abroad will become altogether lop-sided.'

Two decades and twenty UN sessions later, the Cape Town daily, *Die Burger*, decided: 'If we had to keep ourselves busy refuting all the lies preached by the United Nations and its agencies against South Africa, we would have no time and place for anything else.' Truth has been waiting on the doorstep of the United Nations for almost thirty years. She is still waiting. She's used to it. Some day perhaps the United Nations may decide to let her in. It may be too late for South Africa. But it may help others.

44

# 2

# Operation Black-ball

While South Africa is still barely holding on to her seat at the United Nations, she has long ceased to be a member of what used to be the British Commonwealth. The Commonwealth is another organization in which the rise of Afro-Asian voting strength reduced South Africa from the dignified status of founder-member to that of scapegoat and skunk, and eventually led to her virtual expulsion. On 16 March 1961, when South Africa was black-balled at the tenth Commonwealth Prime Ministers' Conference in London, the Afro-Asians commanded six of the eleven votes: but it was not necessary for Ghana, Nigeria, Malaya, Ceylon, India and Pakistan to cast their votes. Most of their work was done for them by an ambitious Canadian Prime Minister seeking popularity and influence among the newly emergent members of the old Commonwealth club.

Eric Louw was South Africa's Foreign Minister at the time and he accompanied Premier Hendrik Verwoerd to London for those historic deliberations. Brilliant and tempestuous, Louw never failed to score a few rabbit punches in his numerous scraps with the press at home and abroad. Cartoonists depicted him as a small baggy-eyed individual with tailor-sized scissors and a fist full of press clippings. Shortly after South Africa's abortive attempt to retain her membership of the Commonwealth on becoming a Republic, Louw held a post mortem on the events leading up to his country's forced withdrawal. Reviewing the role played by Prime Minister Diefenbaker in ousting South Africa, he charged that the Canadian politician had 'pandered' to his home audience.

'He has been losing ground in Canada and is pandering to the anti-South African campaign carried on in the Canadian press as well as in clerical and ultra-liberalistic circles,' said Louw. Immediately the press at large dismissed this claim as yet another 'groundless' accusation. Still, in Toronto the *Globe and Mail* welcomed Mr Louw's charge as 'an accolade' to the Canadian press. His assertion that Canadian government policy on South Africa had been influenced by the Canadian press, said this Toronto paper, should make it possible for 'our diplomats and statesmen to undertake a useful, if humble, role as a voice of moderation among Africa's freedom fighters'.

When South Africa's electorate decided by referendum in October 1960 to replace her monarchical status with a Republican constitution, there were fears that the Afro-Asian majority would use this opportunity to expel her from the Commonwealth. It was expected of members to reapply for membership if they changed their form of government. There were those, however, who expressed the hope that, as had been the case with India, a Republican South Africa would be readmitted without any fuss. After all, they reasoned, the Commonwealth is a family of nations where the stress is supposed to be on areas of agreement rather than disagreement—and although South Africa had been the target at the United Nations of boycotts and sustained attacks from India, Pakistan, Ceylon, Malaya, Ghana and Nigeria, she raised no objection when these countries applied for Commonwealth membership. Finally, there were some who believed that the founding members of the Commonwealth would see to it that South Africa retained her membership.

The Commonwealth had evolved from the British Empire. As far back as the 1880s South African statesman John X. Merriman had used the term 'Commonwealth' to refer to future relationships between the older and more mature members of Britain's Empire and Britain. In 1905 he wrote to Jan Smuts, referring to 'the British Commonwealth of which South Africa as well as Australia, New Zealand and Canada will form part with all the rights of a self-governing community.' This idea of a Commonwealth of Nations appealed to Smuts with his philosophy of holism—a concept that provides for small units developing into bigger wholes, which in turn must grow into larger and ever larger structures without cessation. Thus the unification of

the four provinces in South Africa, the idea of a British Commonwealth of Nations and finally the League of Nations (eventually
reborn as the United Nations), were all favourite projects of
Smuts, the Boer General who became South African Prime
Minister.

As in the formation of the League of Nations and the United
Nations, Smuts played a leading role in the evolution of the
Commonwealth. His successor as Prime Minister, General
J. B. M. Hertzog, was equally enthused by the idea of an informal family relationship emerging from the ashes of the old
British Empire, as long as no member was in any way subservient
to Britain. The Balfour Declaration of 1926 and the Statute of
Westminster in 1934 ensured equality for South Africa. New
Zealand, Australia and Canada. Before, during and for some
time after the Second World War the old Commonwealth
functioned smoothly and effectively. As independent nations
these founding members retained obvious and deep-seated
family ties with Britain and mutual interests with each other.
Then came India, Pakistan and all the others, and a new club
emerged—a multi-racial one which displayed increasing intolerance of viewpoints differing from their own.

Those who expected the new Afro-Asian members of the
Commonwealth to act as South Africa had done when they had
applied for membership and not to raise any objections (despite
serious differences) to South Africa's application for continued
membership as a Republic, made one serious mistake. They
assumed that these new members had the same degree of maturity
as South Africa. The others, who placed their bets on the older
members of the Commonwealth seeing through South Africa's
application in spite of possible severe Afro-Asian objections,
underestimated the power of the press. In Canada at the time
a largely anti-South African press was working their Prime
Minister into a tight corner. Diefenbaker was quite adamant in
his opposition to any ouster move against South Africa until the
Canadian press started intimidating him.

On the day of Diefenbakers's departure from Ottowa to
attend that fateful Commonwealth meeting in March 1961 a
three-column photograph of the doyen of the press corps in
Canada, Charles Lynch, appeared in the local press. In his hand
he held a black ball. The caption read : 'Black Ball Ends Crystal

Balling.' Students planned to hand the black ball to Diefenbaker at Ottawa airport, it was stated, so that he could drop it in the lap of the South African delegation at the Commonwealth conference. They were prevented from doing so by Royal Canadian Air Force guards, and Charles Lynch took over the mission.

This gesture was symbolic of the pressure exerted by the Canadian press on their Prime Minister. It indicated that by 'pandering' to his own press, as Eric Louw put it, Diefenbaker had lost all options but to boot South Africa out of the Commonwealth. Yet this was the very same politician who only a few months before had steadfastly refused to be party to South Africa's expulsion.

In January 1960 Mr Diefenbaker's Minister of External Affairs, Howard Green, told a Vancouver audience that, although Canada disapproved of South Africa's apartheid policy, she did not vote against it in the United Nations 'for fear of disrupting Commonwealth relations'. In Ottawa, Diefenbaker himself remarked that a vote in favour of the UN resolution condemning South Africa could only have been interpreted 'as an unfriendly act toward another member of the Commonwealth'.

The powerful Canadian Labour Congress forwarded a brief to the Prime Minister requesting that the Union of South Africa be dropped from the Commonwealth because of its 'inhuman' apartheid policy. 'We feel extremely uncomfortable in the same company with the Government of South Africa', concluded the CLC. Diefenbaker emphatically defended the right of South Africa to deal with her own domestic problems as she saw fit. He flatly rejected the CLC's demand. 'This is one representation,' he said, 'that will not receive the favourable consideration of the Government.' He furthermore gave an assurance that he would under no circumstances raise the apartheid question at the forthcoming 1960 Commonwealth Prime Ministers' Conference.

In Toronto the men of the press were already moving their artillery into position. On 5 February 1960 the *Globe and Mail* fired the first salvo. 'Mr Macmillan is quite well aware of Commonwealth relationships, and yet, in Cape Town, he chose to ignore them. It cannot have been a simple case of blundering; the British Prime Minister is a polished diplomat whose speeches are models of precision.'

A voluntary decision by South Africa to leave the Commonwealth would not be altogether unwelcome in other member countries, said the *Globe*. It would relieve them of being associated with South Africa's racial policies, and 'greatly strengthen them in the vital struggle to win the allegiance of the uncommitted peoples'. Added the *Toronto Daily Star*: 'Can the Commonwealth afford to offend the Mboyas, the Nyereres and the Abubakars by continuing in close alliance with a government so clearly opposed to their deepest philosophy?'

Sharpeville occurred. The news from South Africa was hideous, with reports of demonstrators being 'mown down' by rifle and machine-gun fire, 'bodies littering' the streets, and hospitals 'filled' with wounded. The death of sixty-nine Black demonstrators unlocked the doors of a huge armoury for the Canadian press battalions. Most newspapers, running short of ammunition at the time, helped themselves freely to this unexpected supply. Few were the voices of moderation. One of these few, the *Fredericton Gleaner* of New Brunswick, pointed out that 'every time the forces of law and order are placed on the defensive, the world is deluged with news reports slanted in favour of the law-breakers. So it is today in South Africa. Every Negro demonstrator against the laws of the Union is inculpable and every policeman a headbreaker. That is the tenor of the stories we receive—and publish from big news agencies. Take this despatch from Cape Town: "Troops and police clubbed hundreds of Negroes in Cape Town area today when the Negroes failed to join a native back-to-work movement. Police also staged house-to-house raids and shooting was heard in one Negro township." '

Asked the *Gleaner*: 'Why are police doing this—if they were doing it? The despatch does not say. It gives a grim story from the rioters' point of view and lets it go at that. Granted the South African situation is a bad one. The majority of Canadians are opposed to the policy of apartheid. But this gives more reason than ever for straight unbiased news reporting. And that, here in Canada, we are not getting. We trust our readers are searching between the lines as we are.'

There is, however, a time in war when reason must give way to unabated emotionalism. The *Toronto Daily Star*, incensed by the detention and deportation of its Foreign News Editor, Norman Phillips, from South Africa, was in the process of enlisting private citizens : 'Canadians might find it more effective to flood Prime Minister Diefenbaker's office with letters demanding official protest to South Africa and that he personally express Canada's indignation at the Commonwealth Prime Minister's Conference.'

Diefenbaker later admitted that citizens did respond. But, he added, there had been no disproportionate number of letters either favouring or opposing the Canadian Government's attitude of non-interference. The *Daily Star* noted with regret that 'the Prime Minister has weakened his own personal prestige by his use of procedural stratagem to avert a vote [on apartheid] in the House of Commons.'

Announced the *Globe and Mail*: 'This newspaper has urged that Prime Minister Diefenbaker speak up for Canada in making it clear that his country cannot condone South African government policies. We have also urged, however, that individuals and organizations across the country demonstrate their concern.' In another editorial it urged the Canadian Parliament to express Canadian opinion on apartheid in such a way that it 'should, if anything, harden the determination of the Nationalist Government to create a republic, and perhaps leave the Commonwealth'.

At Milner Park showgrounds in Johannesburg, South Africa was celebrating her fiftieth birthday. The Union's Prime Minister delivered a touching and sincere opening speech. Minutes after he sat down a deranged wealthy Witwatersrand farmer confronted Dr Hendrik Verwoerd and fired several shots from point-blank range. The Prime Minister miraculously escaped death.

In the Canadian press there were expressions of regret coupled with insinuations that this was the inevitable result of the policy of apartheid. A near tragedy for South Africa became a pretext for malice. A daily in Fort William even protested against heads of state sympathizing, then conceded that 'protocol calls for messages of this kind perhaps'. The *Toronto Daily Star* summed up: 'He who sows the wind must in the end reap the whirlwind.'

The 'oust South Africa' movement reached its peak shortly before the 1960 Commonwealth Conference attended by Foreign Minister Louw in place of the injured South African Premier. 'John Diefenbaker should not compromise Canadian principles and jeopardize the goodwill of the non-White members,' said the *Telegram*. 'To speak out assumes the nature of a moral duty', declared the *Montreal Star*. Diefenbaker 'may be out of touch with public opinion in Canada', added the *Sudbury Star*. The *London Evening Free Press* prayed that South Africa would decide to leave the Commonwealth of her own accord. This, it noted, would eliminate the necessity of booting her out. The *Winnipeg Tribune* assured its Prime Minister that 'no amount of silence would have slowed down the process that has now begun'.

Diefenbaker stood firm. He told the Canadian House of Commons that his government did not intend to make a diplomatic protest or intervene in any other way in South African affairs. He simply deplored the loss of lives at Sharpeville. In May 1960, before he left for the Commonwealth parley in London, he further clarified his stand : 'I fear for the future of the Commonwealth if, while never failing to make clear the viewpoint of each of us, the Prime Ministers' conference should become the judge and jury of the conduct of member-nations.'

He cited ex-Prime Ministers MacKenzie King and Louis St Laurent as having subscribed to his own view that 'there should be nothing done among the member-nations to cause division and dissension'. He hinted that someone in the Commonwealth might equally dislike Canada's restriction of coloured immigrants and its treatment of the Indians. 'What is to be gained,' asked Diefenbaker, 'by kicking South Africa out of the Commonwealth?'

The press of Canada lost the first round. Diefenbaker refused to interfere in the internal affairs of a fellow Commonwealth nation at the 1960 conference. But this initial set-back did not discourage the press corps. In fact, it lead to new offensives. More editorials. Articles. Letters to the Editor. Mr Diefenbaker, they maintained, should take heed of the 'militant concern' over apartheid and South Africa. At the end of 1960 he did. Canada reversed her position on South Africa at the United Nations. For the first time she voted in support of a resolution condemning a fellow Commonwealth member.

The stage was set for the next move—South Africa's expulsion from the Commonwealth in March 1961 when she was expected to reapply for membership as a republic. 'There is considerable pressure being brought to bear on the Canadian Government to refuse South Africa membership of the Commonwealth', announced one Canadian daily. To cut ties with South Africa 'would strengthen the Commonwealth', said another. Mr Diefenbaker bore the key which could lock the door in the South African Government's face. And he had no option. 'For reasons of domestic and international politics,' he could not align himself with South Africa in the face of opposition from the African and Asian members. 'The so-called Whites are a tiny minority.'

The *Toronto Telegram* News Service syndicated a column called 'Pulse Survey of Canada' to convince the Prime Minister and others that 'informed opinion' would be even more strongly in favour of the expulsion of South Africa if there was a schism between White and Coloured members on the membership issue. 'Pulse Survey', it was claimed, reflected the opinions of 'educators, editors, businessmen and labour leaders across Canada'.

One Canadian businessman who planned to express his support for South Africa's continued membership, decided to cancel his speech in the face of severe criticism. 'The cancellation of what might have been a touchy speech, in itself an innocuous act, suggests that attitudes exist in our midst which are not conducive to the atmosphere of freedom which we cherish for Canada', observed a newspaper.

On 6 March 1961 Mr G. M. Hobart, President of the Consolidated Paper Corporation in Montreal, had an interview with the *Natal Daily News* in Durban, South Africa. He told the *Daily News* that as a visitor from Canada he had had a completely wrong impression of South Africa's internal situation. He blamed the press for creating this impression. On the following day the *Toronto Telegram* reminded Mr Hobart that 'as President of a newsprint company, he is biting the hand that feeds his company when he criticizes the press'.

Vancouver columnist Harold Weir was one notable traitor to the 'black-ball' campaign. It seemed to be imperative to look a little more closely into the Whites' side of the case, said Weir. 'I am well aware that to even hint that the White Government [in South Africa] has a case, represents an unpopular and minority viewpoint. But when I find myself becoming too impressed with the popular, majority viewpoints, I am moved to remember that it was an overwhelming majority that cried: Release Barabas!'

In Ottawa columnist Patrick Best pointed out that 'Canada's leading daily newspapers have left no doubt that the dominant issue at the current Commonwealth Prime Ministers' Conference in London is the policy of racial apartheid'. And they were unanimous in their view that 'a policy which promotes White supremacy was repugnant in a multi-racial family of nations'. Said Best: 'The onus was placed on Prime Minister Diefenbaker to take the lead, as head of one of the senior dominions, in bringing the issue to the fore at the London conference.'

According to the *Montreal Star*, Diefenbaker 'carries with him the onerous burden of declaring the feelings of a second senior member of the Commonwealth about racial discrimination'. 'If he should go further,' said the *Winnipeg Free Press*, 'and lead a movement to keep the Republic of South Africa out of the Commonwealth unless she mends her ways, he will still be speaking for many people in Canada.' 'Diefenbaker can be counted on to stand with his colored brothers', assured the *Vancouver Sun*. 'There could be greater losses than the loss of South Africa', decided the *Victoria Daily Times*.

The Commonwealth, 'though necessarily tolerant of differences among members, cannot harbor the rampant contradiction of South African apartheid', insisted the *Toronto Daily Star*. If Diefenbaker 'forces the West to match words with deeds, he can win for himself a historic role as trusted friend in Afro-Asian eyes'. The *Toronto Telegram* argued that 'any nation that cannot sign the Declaration of Human Rights does not qualify for membership in the Commonwealth'. Added the *Globe and Mail*: 'South Africa has no place in the Commonwealth.' If she refused to leave of her own accord, she must be requested to do so.

On the day of his departure for London in March 1961, Diefenbaker received final instructions from the *Globe and Mail*. It is to be hoped, the *Globe* said, that Mr Diefenbaker will speak more plainly on the subject in London than he did in Ottawa; and that he will oppose the racial policies of the South African Government not simply as an individual, but as Prime Minister of Canada. 'The resistance of only one member-nation is necessary for the exclusion of South Africa; and we believe that such resistance should come from Canada.'

At the Canadian Club in London, shortly before the Conference opened, Diefenbaker once again argued that the Commonwealth should 'not sit in judgement of any of its members', somewhat hesitatingly and less convincingly than before. The *Globe and Mail* was despondent : 'Our Prime Minister in fact now seems firmly aligned with the group at the Conference which is opposing any move to exclude South Africa from the Commonwealth.'

Next to Dr Verwoerd himself, British Prime Minister Harold Macmillan worked zealously for months to prevent the break. When the parley started the British press gave Dr Verwoerd a fifty-fifty chance of success. Diefenbaker's speech at the Canadian Club made the odds somewhat more favourable for Verwoerd. The other senior members, Australia and New Zealand, were already firmly behind South Africa's continued membership.

South Africa's application was brought up for discussion. The Afro-Asians grasped the opportunity to attack the policy of apartheid. Verwoerd had expected opposition from the Afro-Asian members, but according to Australian Premier Robert Menzies, it was Diefenbaker of Canada who made the first attack. 'He came,' said Menzies, 'armed with a resolution of his parliament and presented his views with immense emotion.'

The South African Prime Minister explained apartheid, answered numerous questions and gave full information on its aims and implementation. He even went out of his way to meet the demands of his opponents who insisted that their views on apartheid be aired in the final *communiqué*. The Afro-Asians were not satisfied. Forcefully led by Diefenbaker they insisted that the final declaration should subscribe to the principle of multi-racialism as binding on each member. They knew that South Africa would never be able to consent. She withdrew. Tom Stacey of the London *Sunday Times* remarked with surprise that Diefenbaker 'moralized more prolixly and piously than any of the Afro-Asians'.

Operation Black-ball succeeded. On the chilly morning of 17 March 1961 John Diefenbaker returned to Ottawa. Hundreds of well-wishers turned up in thick overcoats to meet their idol at the airport. 'The Commonwealth is stronger than ever before because of the central theme of non-discrimination that ran through all our meetings,' he told a crowd of enthusiastic newsmen. Later, in the House of Commons, he explained that if the Commonwealth had approved South Africa's continued membership it would have meant condoning apartheid. 'I suggested at the Conference that, if we were to agree that South African membership in the Commonwealth was a mere formality under its changed constitutional status, we would be approving policies abhorred and unequivocally condemned by Canadians as a whole.'

On the dimly lit shelves of the parliamentary library, further along the marble corridors of the very same building, were records of a speech he made less than a year before. Freshly bound in neat dark green Hansard cloth, it contained passages like the following: 'I fear for the future of the Commonwealth if . . . the Prime Ministers' Conference should become the judge and jury of the conduct of member-nations. What is to be gained by kicking South Africa out of the Commonwealth?' Nothing should be done among member-nations to cause division and dissention, he said then. But this was 1960. Records of the past. John Diefenbaker was in no mood to look back. It was a time for rejoicing.

'The Commonwealth has been saved', exclaimed the *Telegram*. 'Diefenbaker has emerged as a front-rank leader of the Commonwealth in its transition to a new multi-racial form, and his success has confirmed his rank as a world statesman.' The *Vancouver Sun* praised their Prime Minister 'who bore the brunt, bore the resentments of his fellow white prime ministers who would have temporized'. He had showed moral courage of a high order and his fellow Canadians would not deny him their tribute.

'This week has been one of tension and anxiety', admitted a relieved *Montreal Star*. 'For Canadians the tension was increased for a time by the prospect that the Prime Minister would align himself with those forces willing to appease. For his consistent stand he deserves nothing but praise.' 'In London,' said the *Ottawa Journal*, 'Mr Diefenbaker acted as he thought a good Canadian Commonwealth man should act. He now has the absolute assurance that other good Canadian Commonwealth men in other parties agree with him.' Predicted the *Globe and Mail*: 'The present Commonwealth members will return to the United Nations with an entirely new status.'

There were few discordant notes amidst the chorus of praise.

55

The *Fredericton Gleaner* provided one. It accused Diefenbaker's admirers of 'heresy hunting'. Another, the *Kingston Whig-Standard,* questioned the validity of the argument that the Canadian Prime Minister acted according to the 'will of his people'. Said the *Whig-Standard* : 'Nobody knows anything about the "will of the Canadian people" except that there is no such thing. To use terms such as this is a convenient way of blanking out all the sincere argument which was used against what Mr Diefenbaker did in London.'

A few weeks before John Diefenbaker's departure for London the *Telegram* 'Pulse Survey' had told him that 'informed opinion' favoured South Africa's expulsion. Some weeks after South Africa's forced withdrawal the Canadian Institute of Public Opinion undertook another poll.

'Mr Diefenbaker's stand, credited by many commentators as a deciding factor in the crisis, is supported in principle by about three in ten of those who have heard something about it', the Canadian Institute concluded. 'On the other hand, about four in ten hold an opposing point of view. Just under four [the rest] in ten are not aware of the development at all.'

Diefenbaker always felt very strongly about human rights and the dignity of man. Like many true believers in this field, his doctrine of human rights was, however, an abstract one. As Prime Minister he issued a Declaration of Human Rights, duplicated by commercial concerns for free distribution to schools. But problems affecting the underprivileged Indians and Eskimos remained unchanged. Discriminatory practices in Canada continued, while he focused on racism abroad—especially the alleged racism of South Africa.

And the Afro-Asians who applauded Diefenbaker's tenacious stand against South Africa on the grounds of alleged racism, how did they perform at home? India with a rigid caste system and millions of third-class citizens called 'untouchables', Ceylon with her stateless Tamils, Ghana, a dictatorship and Nigeria at that stage on the verge of a bloody clash between her major tribes? Said South Africa Premier Verwoerd to the Indian Prime Minister during the deliberations : 'Within ten years we will stamp out illiteracy on the part of our Blacks, but you won't do so in fifty years.'

'The inexorable logic of our situation forced Diefenbaker's

Government into this position,' stated veteran newsman John Bird in the *Toronto Star* at the time, 'however much it may have wriggled and twisted and turned in the past two years on this very issue.'

Two years later John Diefenbaker lost the general election in Canada. The Commonwealth lost its last 'model' Black democracy in a night of terror which left the Nigerian Prime Minister, Tafewa Balewa, and his trusted aides in shallow graves near Lagos. Then followed the Biafran War and more than two million victims—Black killed by Black. Kenya and Uganda forced tens of thousands of Indians to leave. India and Pakistan fought over borders. Then came Bangladesh and another few hundred thousand victims.

In 1961, shortly after the London *débâcle*, the Associated Press had reported from Johannesburg: 'South Africa's largest English newspaper warned that the days of Prime Minister Hendrik Verwoerd's white supremacy government are numbered. The English press in South Africa suggests that, with a rapid deterioration of this country's political fortunes, Dr Verwoerd is losing his grip on affairs.' Early 1966 found Hendrik Verwoerd still solidly in control of an economically buoyant South Africa, another spectacular election victory behind him.

In Canada in 1966 the debate in the House revolved around —the latest problem in the Commonwealth—independent Rhodesia. The Canadian Prime Minister, Lester Pearson, insisted that joint Commonwealth action was needed to crush 'white supremacy' there. Opposition leader Diefenbaker rose laboriously from his seat. This question of Rhodesia, he argued, was an internal matter for Britain to solve. The Commonwealth should not interfere. But what about London in March 1961, Mr Diefenbaker? someone asked. Were you not instrumental in the expulsion of South Africa because of apartheid? Replied John Diefenbaker: 'At no time did I indirectly or at all support the removal of South Africa. At no time was such a stand taken.'

Twisting, wriggling and turning, John Diefenbaker was trying to win back a principle which he had conceded to the Canadian press five years earlier. In a letter to the *Toronto Globe and Mail* on 23 March 1961 the late Arthur Barlow, a veteran South African parliamentarian, concluded with this indictment: 'Prime Minister Hendrik Verwoerd has stood by his principles; your

Prime Minister has not done so.' Had Barlow known the full extent of the press campaign that forced Diefenbaker to forsake his principle of 'non-interference' in the affairs of other Commonwealth members, he might have sympathized with the Canadian Prime Minister instead.

Also on 23 March 1961 Prime Minister Verwoerd reviewed the London events in a speech in the Cape Town House of Assembly. The new Commonwealth, he pointed out, was quite different from the old one. Previously it had been a true family of nations with blood ties and common interests. Now it had become a congregation of nations with only one thing in common—they had all been ruled by Britain at one stage or another. 'The Commonwealth has changed into something very similar to the United Nations on a small scale,' Dr Verwoerd said.

In 1974 the late Dr Verwoerd's National Party was still in power with an even larger majority than before. At the helm was John Vorster, who further increased his party's comfortable margin in Parliament. While the rest of the world was suffering from serious inflationary problems, South Africa was experiencing only relatively mild symptoms. In Ottawa the Commonwealth Prime Ministers gathered for a twelve-day parley—thirty-two of them, including those from Malta and Malaya, Trinidad and Tanzania, Cyprus and Ceylon. A motley group presided over by Britain, which was frequently deserted even by old faithfuls like Australia and New Zealand.

As an ordinary opposition back-bencher, Mr Diefenbaker must have been quite green-eyed watching those two super-socialists from down south—Prime Minister Gough Whitlam of Australia and Norman Kirk of New Zealand—playing up to the large Afro-Asian gallery. Even Canada's Prime Minister, Pierre Trudeau, looked amateurish in his attempts to win friends and influence Prime Ministers from the Third World. It was obvious that Black Africa ran the conference, and that General Gowon of Nigeria was the real voice of authority rather than Britain's Prime Minister, Edward Heath. Instead of calling the tune, Heath and his Foreign Minister Sir Alec Douglas-Home, found themselves pinned to the wall on the Rhodesian and South African 'questions'. Heath actually spoke in despondent fashion about the 'deplorable' practice of 'Britain-bashing' at the conference.

South African newsman Raymond Heard reported from Ottawa. 'To put it bluntly,' he said, 'the new socialist Governments of Australia and New Zealand are ganging up with the Black Africans, led by OAU (Organization for African Unity) Chairman General Yakubu Gowon of Nigeria, to tighten the screws on South Africa, Rhodesia and Portugal. This has further isolated Britain's Prime Minister, Mr Edward Heath, from what must be called the mainstream of new Commonwealth thinking.' Mr Heath maintained that there was nothing more the Commonwealth could do in practical (as opposed to theoretical) terms to end White rule in Southern Africa. Added Heard: 'Nobody except the light-weight Prime Minister of Fiji has spoken out yet against the racist policy of Uganda's General Amin towards the Asians.'

At the Ottawa Summit Britain received explicit instructions on how to handle Rhodesia. Afterwards an American liberal journal asked John Hutchinson to write an article about this aspect of the Commonwealth parley. Hutchinson, a Visiting Professor of International Relations at John Hopkins University, is a renowned egalitarian who despises any hint of racial supremacy. He replied as follows: 'You asked for my observations on the proposal, made at the last Commonwealth Summit, for a Commonwealth Force to be stationed in Rhodesia for ten years to keep the peace and, presumably, to usher in a democratic age.

'. . . The mind expands at the idea. General Amin of Uganda could administer massacres. Prime Minister Forbes Burnham of Guyana might give a course on inter-racial affection. Prime Minister Errol Barrow of Barbados, who apparently is not afraid of bloodshed in Rhodesia, could advise on the Mafia concession, a major perk in the Caribbean. I don't quite know what Prime Minister Gough Whitlam of Australia might do, since he is busy analysing other governments, but perhaps he could squeeze in a lecture on "Aspects of Aboriginal Freedom"; it wouldn't take long, since there are only aspects to deal with.

'We are, of course in the politics of the absurd,' noted this liberal professor. 'Rhodesia seems to be fine sport for a slack morning at the Summit. I respect the good intentions of most of the gentlemen of the Commonwealth, but they are short of brains and modesty.' These days Rhodesia often features at Commonwealth meetings, but never in isolation. It is always

59

presented as part of the 'problem of Southern Africa'.

The Commonwealth has indeed become the UN on a small scale. It plays the double-standard game with great ease and expertise—ignoring Uganda's crimes against the Indians, side-tracking the Nigerian war and its mass-scale killings, turning a blind eye towards discriminatory practices in India, Canada and a host of other member countries, while pouncing on the 'racist crimes' of southern Africa. It has an Afro-Asian majority and several Western fellow travellers placating the Afro-Asians. The Commonwealth is the UN in miniature but for one thing—South Africa is not there any longer to listen to its abuse.

# 3

# Only a Torch

'Only a torch for burning, no hammer for building?
Take our thanks, then, and—thyself away.'

CARLYLE

In December South Africa's townspeople rusticate. Small resort
hotels unbutton their freshly painted shutters. Forlorn beaches
suddenly blossom into colourful umbrella-specked community
centres. Newspapers dismount from their political horses. Pictures
of smiling suntanned faces and pretty girls in brief bathing
costumes abound. Serious affairs of state are left behind in
Pretoria.

December 1957, however, found the legal machinery of South
Africa still in top gear. On the fifth day of that hot midsummer
month detectives called on a hundred and forty households.
Black, White, Indian and Coloured were taken from their homes
across the country to the nearest magistrates' courts, remanded
and taken to railway stations and airfields.

During the next few days they arrived in Johannesburg. One
hundred and fifty-six in all. A Black professor, a White book-
maker, a Member of Parliament, three clergymen, two truck-
drivers, eight lawyers and seven doctors. Men and women from
all walks of life. They were charged with treason. These
people, summed up prosecutor Van Niekerk, incited and prepared for the overthrow of the State by revolutionary methods
involving violence.

A fortnight they waited in Johannesburg's Central Prison.
There were far too many to fit into an ordinary courtroom, so a
special one was prepared in Johannesburg's military Drill Hall.
On 19 December the leadership of the so-called National
Liberation Front faced the Bench. They represented the African

61

National Congress (ANC); the South African Indian Congress (SAIC); the South African Congress of Trade Unions (SACTU); the South African Coloured People's Organization (SACPO); the Congress of Democrats (COD); and the South African Communist Party (SACP).

These were the organizations which promised the populace of South Africa Utopia on a collective basis. 'We the people of South Africa declare for all our country and the world to know . . .' This was the preamble to the Freedom Charter they had issued at Kliptown two years before. 'We the people . . .' The ANC, the strongest arm of this octopus, claimed a paid-up membership of 50,000—only ½ per cent of the Black or Bantu population of South Africa.

On the third day of the treason trial all the accused were released on bail and the court adjourned. The hearings resumed on 9 January 1958. From Britain came Mr Gerald Gardiner, QC, to observe the preliminary proceedings 'on behalf of the three political lawyers' societies'. He came, in fact, as a representative of the London-based Defence and Aid Fund, operating under the aegis of Christian Action. Sporting a few prominent Communists on its executive and Canon Collins at the top of the table, Christian Action through its Defence and Aid subsidiary picked up the tab for the treason trialists' defence and keep in Johannesburg.

Many months later and millions of words after that eventful December all the accused were acquitted. Piet Beyleveld (41), Afrikaner businessman; Jack Hodgson (47), former Secretary of the Springbok Legion; Mrs Helen Joseph, English secretary of a Johannesburg medical aid society; Nelson Mandela (39), Bantu attorney; Walter Sisulu (45), Bantu organiser; Joe Slovo (31), White barrister, and Mrs Ruth (First) Slovo (32), White journalist and wife of Joe; Oliver Tambo (40), Bantu solicitor; Mrs Sonia Bunting (34), White housewife; Ben Turok, White member of the Cape Provincial Council; Len Lee-Warden (44), White MP.

Ex-Chief Albert J. Luthuli, President of the ANC, was among the first batch of acquittals. 'It is with mixed feelings,' he said, 'that I received the news of my release; the truth is that I would be happier to see the whole thing through with my comrades.' He assured a journalist friend, Anthony Sampson: 'If I were convinced that Congress (ANC) was working for Moscow, I would definitely resign.'

In the Drill Hall he shared sandwiches and chairs with Comrades Hodgson, Slovo and others. Anthony Sampson, in his book *The Treason Cage*, says categorically : 'All the twenty-three Europeans who were arrested were members of the Congress of Democrats and most of them were Communists or fellow travellers.'

Luthuli did not resign, then or later, although their mission became as clear as the hammer and sickle on the Russian flag. As President of the ANC he was supposed to know the history of his own organization. As far back as 1936 the Secretary-General of the ANC was a Communist, J. B. Marks. Prominent in organizing strikes in South Africa, he later moved to Russia where, on his death, he was acclaimed by the Communists for his work in South Africa. In 1949 Moses Kotane, then Secretary-General of the South African Communist Party, became Secretary-General of the ANC. A year later the Communist Party was driven underground. Kotane also shared sandwiches with Luthuli, but the chief did not resign.

White Communist domination of the ANC was one of the serious charges raised by Robert Sobukwe when he pied-pipered a following of young militant men away from the Congress in 1958. The newly formed Pan-African Congress preached Black Power. Other races should be exterminated or sent packing, said Witwatersrand university lecturer Robert Sobukwe.

In its infant days during the mid-fifties the Liberal Party avoided contact with the ANC. Noted Anthony Sampson : 'There were reasons enough for the Liberals, who were generally people with ideals and integrity to shun Congress . . . Its demand for a universal franchise was alarming to anyone who had watched a beer-hall mob; its speeches, particularly on foreign affairs, smacked of crude Communist dogma . . . its members included extreme nationalists, opportunists and Communists—undesirable bedfellows for respectable European Liberals.'

The South African Liberal Party preferred to court the White electorate. It did all the things parliamentary groupings were supposed to do. It arranged meetings, it entered candidates for general elections and it held fund-raising functions. But it never won a single seat in Parliament or the Provincial Councils or even at the municipal level of local government. It remained a somewhat off-beam and immature speck on the fringe of South African parliamentary politics, its political ideology rejected by South Africans.

Rebuffed and disillusioned, tired of waiting in the wings, the Liberal Party gradually drifted towards the ANC and its associated pressure groups. Like a worm-infested apple it was quietly eaten away from inside by the ANC and its military wing, Umkonto we Sizwe, by the so-called African Resistance Movement and the banned Communist Party. When it dropped from the tree in the mid-sixties it splattered apart, revealing a sickly sight.

Sitting in the small Liberal Party craft with his hand tightly clasped around a broken rudder was Alan Paton, former Principal of Diepkloof Reformatory for Blacks and author of *Cry the Beloved Country*. Paton went through the motions in good faith, believing rather naively that he, as leader of the Liberals, was setting the course. In the meantime the real course was determined not by him or any other *bona-fide* office-bearer. It was set by a strong undercurrent of which he appeared blissfully unaware. Some years later, when he did discover it, the South African Liberal Party was already shipwrecked and helpless.

On 24 April 1958 a report published in the *Johannesburg Star* quoted the South African Commissioner of Police, Major-General C. I. Rademeyer, as saying : 'Edgar Hoover might just as well have been the Commissioner of Police in South Africa, writing about Communist activities here and the experiences of the South African police in dealing with the problem.' It was not a very prominent item. Simply a South African police official commenting on the advance copy of Hoover's *Masters of Deceit*, which was sent to him by the United States Embassy in Pretoria.

Referring to the FBI Chief's exposure of Communist infiltration tactics, sabotage attempts and mass agitation methods in the United States, Major-General Rademeyer added : 'I can go further and say that, if you change the names in this book, the picture precisely fits the South African situation.' Shocking? Few cared. Hardly a ripple of comment. It is true that South Africa had its Communists—eleven years earlier the US House Committee on Foreign Affairs gave 'world rating' to fourteen of them. But infiltration and sabotage? Simply impossible. Not in South Africa.

Then came 1960. The fiftieth birthday of the Union of South Africa. A year of festivity. But even before the candles were lit British Prime Minister Harold Macmillan introduced a sour note in a speech before the joint Houses of Parliament in Cape Town. In what later became known as the 'wind of change' speech, Macmillan advised South Africa's parliamentarians to take account of the wave of Black nationalism sweeping across Africa. Answered his host, South African Premier Verwoerd: 'The tendency in Africa for nations to become independent and, at the same time, the need to do justice to all, does not only mean being just to the Black man of Africa but also being just to the White man of Africa.'

Trying to ensure that this would be the last celebration of White South Africa committed to Western ideals were both the ANC and PAC, assisted and guided by a string of White Communists and Coloured and Indian satellite groupings. One of the pamphlets distributed among Black communities stated boldly: 'The present capitalistic South African state must be completely destroyed and a people's state must be built up. Our comrades will want that we wrest the country from our oppressors with armed force and that, after victory, we march on to the establishment of the South African People's Republic.'

At Sharpeville, near Vereeniging, members of the Pan African Congress told the Black inhabitants to demonstrate at the nearest police station without their reference books. Those who refused, and there were many, were dealt with so severely that they could not help but change their minds. At 1 p.m. on 21 March there were between 15,000 and 20,000 demonstrators outside the small Sharpeville police station. The police tried to reason. Then more demonstrators arrived. The crowds started throwing stones. The advance group of demonstrators broke through a gate separating the small contingent of policemen from the threatening masses. The police opened fire. Sixty-nine Black demonstrators were killed, many more wounded.

Two months earlier it was Cato Manor, near Durban. Four White and five non-White policemen battered to death by a mob. In Langa, near Cape Town, the driver of a news car was stoned to death. Elsewhere several Black dissenters were tortured and maimed because they dared to oppose the leadership of this insurrection.

But these were all mere 'incidents', while Sharpeville was a 'massacre'. Around the world it echoed. A brief twenty-second salvo of gun-shots which gave birth to a myth. Today in a dozen or more countries left-wing groups still 'commemorate' Sharpeville every year on 21 March—a homage not accorded to the millions who perished during Stalin's Great Terror, the more than a million who died in Nigeria's Biafran war or the several hundred thousand who were massacred in cold blood in Burundi, Sudan and several other African states.

On 9 April 1960 a deranged White farmer sneaked through the dense crowd at the Milner Park exhibition ground in Johannesburg and fired several shots at the South African Premier. Dr Verwoerd miraculously escaped death and recovered in hospital. Six weeks later, on 31 May, when the South African leader appeared in Bloemfontein to deliver the main address at the fiftieth birthday celebration of the Union of South Africa, tranquillity reigned after firm action by the Government against the forces of subversion. On the surface at least.

The emergency measures introduced to cope with the torrent of terror unleashed by the ANC and the PAC, together with the banned Communist Party and other White-dominated subversive groups, were lifted on 11 May. This signalled a return to normality and the departure of many leading sensation-seekers of the world press. Canadian journalist Norman Phillips, who came to South Africa with instructions from the *Toronto Star* to concentrate on 'blood and guts' material, left on a deportation order after spending a few days in prison. The authorities were not in the mood to tolerate a journalist who wrote first-hand accounts of imaginary violence in Cape Town while living it up in a Durban hotel room 700 miles away.

Phillips was only one out of a crowd of truth-twisters. Terms like 'tens of thousands' and 'thousands' became customary in describing any demonstration against the Government, although some of these demonstrations hardly delivered more than a hundred participants. The *New York Times* found out the hard way just exactly how reliable these reports were. On 6 April 1960 it expressed indignation at continuing reports that Blacks in Cape Town were 'being forced back to work by police use of clubs, whips and guns'—which were, in fact, the crude methods used by the ring-leaders of the 'resistance movements' to *prevent* Blacks from crossing the picket lines. On 21 April the *New York Times* admitted that 'the large mass of Africans ignored the strike call and flocked back to work and school'. No apology for its editorial of 6 April, however.

Press pundits in 'leading liberal journals' across the globe had no problem in picking sides. Their sympathies and support were entirely with the 'popular uprising' of Black South Africa and very much against the 'White regime'. Not once did it occur to them to have a good hard look at their heroes and what they really stood for. Even if they did discover that the revolutionary leadership and their small following were programmed and powered by Moscow, it would not have made one iota of difference. Hatred for Premier Verwoerd and his Government was such that even the Devil in opposition would have sufficed.

The usually reserved London *Times* was given to terms like 'stink in the nostrils' in airing its views about the set-up in 'unhappy' South Africa. Verwoerd, it said, was 'a liar' and his policy 'manifestly bankrupt'. Across the Atlantic, the *New York Times* announced that the 'police killed, by *official* count, seventy-two Africans and wounded 184'. It added: 'The *real* figures are doubtless a bit higher.' In the same thinly veiled fashion the *New York Times* exploited the terrible Coalbrook mine disaster where 435 Whites and Blacks perished in a coal-mine collapse. Commenting on the fact that the vast majority were Blacks, the *Times* said: 'There is no suggestion that carelessness or exploitation caused the Coalbrook collapse. But at a time of exacerbated racial feelings in the Union, the disaster is bound to serve as a glaring searchlight, showing up the murky and foreboding atmosphere of apartheid ... '

The lifting of the emergency measures on 11 May 1960 marked the end of subversive South Africa's onslaught on the cities—and the departure of a disappointed world press corps. But there was still a violent campaign being waged in the rural areas. In the Transkei chiefs and headmen were molested. Several murders took place. At the conclusion of one of the subsequent trials counsel for the defence called Mr Swartz, a Black lawyer. Orders came from 'head office', he explained. And 'head office' meant White Communists.

Noted one observer in a South African Sunday newspaper, *Dagbreek en Sondagnuus*: 'There is legislation against sedition, public violence, unlawful gatherings, inciting of racialism, for the suppression of Communism, the Public Safety Act and others. All these laws resulted from the activities of Communists and their satellites and every one covers a certain field. But as we shall see the whole field has not yet been covered.

'. . . Take as an example the case of two Bantu men, tools of the Communists, who are caught at night at a power pylon. The one is sawing through the power pylon with a hacksaw while the other is keeping guard some distance away with a firearm in his hand. As the law reads today, one can be charged with malicious injury to property and the other with possession of an unlicensed firearm . . . '

The General Law Amendment Act of 1962 corrected the situation. It defined sabotage. It provided for the proper punishment of saboteurs. It included provisions to crush Communist publications. It introduced house arrest. This, explained the Justice Minister, would not withhold the right of those placed under house arrest to perform their daily work.

Member of Opposition : 'What happens if he is a traveller?'

Minister of Justice : 'In that case he should join the United Party [opposition]; then he will be a traveller with out any destination.' (Laughter)

A moment of laughter in the House to break the dead seriousness of the subject. Outside, processions and protest. Smears from abroad—'The end of the rule of law', 'The flame of freedom had been extinguished', 'the last vestige of individual freedom is being whittled away by a police state government'. The first of many telegrams of protest came from Walter Sisulu, still in hiding.

'If one studies the agitation made against this Bill,' noted Justice Minister Vorster, 'it becomes clear that the people who are opposed to the Bill in the first place—and let me say this, that they have every reason to be opposed to it—are the Communists.'

South Africa's far-left, ably supported by sympathizers at home and abroad, invoked the usual shibboleths and catchphrases. The rights of man, human rights, dignity, individual freedom. Such was the stormy birth of the Sabotage Act. The

68

introduction of the 90-day clause and the 180-day measure was no less eventful and stormy.

On the one hand a group of desperadoes, no different from those who launched the Russian Revolution in the name of individual freedom and equality only to incarcerate and liquidate even the very thought of freedom once they came to power. On the other hand, a Western democratic government finding itself increasingly forced to bend democratic principles in its endeavours to contain the spread of the deadly Red weed.

'We are dealing with an enemy which does not fight according to the Queensberry Rules,' said Vorster. In the early morning hours of a November day in 1962 an armed band attacked the police station at Paarl. On the way they hacked to death two White youngsters and plundered property. Enter POQO— military wing of Sobukwe's militant PAC, now under the leadership of Potlako Leballo while the former university lecturer is restricted.

In the Eastern Cape another band of POQO men converged on two roadside trailers and set them on fire. A family of four Whites was hacked, battered and shot to death. In the second trailer a young single man was cremated. There were also several attempts to kill Black authorities in the territory. Arrests followed. One of the state witnesses was slaughtered. His murderers received the death penalty.

Again protests from abroad. A special plea signed by the Secretary-General of the United Nations was addressed to the South African Government. Spare the lives of the men sentenced to die because of their 'opposition to apartheid', U Thant demanded. This was one plea which did not receive consideration.

Early in 1963 a pamphlet appeared in mail-boxes in White suburbs. Issued by the banned ANC, it read in part: 'LISTEN, WHITE MAN! Five Whites were murdered in the Transkei, another hacked to death in Langa . . . Sabotage erupts every other week throughout the country, now here, now there. The Whites are turning vicious and panicky . . . At this rate, within a year or two South Africa will be embroiled in the second, bloodier, more furious Algerian war. SABOTAGE AND MURDERS MULTIPLIED LAST YEAR. SABOTAGE AND MURDER WILL NOT CEASE.'

But the whole field of terror was not left to POQO alone. Since 1961 the ANC had had its own militant wing operating under the name Umkonto we Sizwe—'Spear of the Nation'. Carrying out a spate of sabotage acts on 16 December 1961, Umkonto made certain that nobody would mistake it for some other organization. It posted placards to announce its birth. To the in-group the Umkonto High Command was known as MK.

On a July afternoon in 1964 two men of South Africa's Security Police drove to Lilliesleaf Farm near Rivonia, Johannesburg, in a borrowed dry cleaners' van. In the back, huddled together under a blanket, were fourteen colleagues and a police dog. The small vehicle jerked to a halt in front of a modern tile-roofed mansion. Suddenly the police were all over the farmyard, running and opening doors.

Thus ended the days of MK. Trapped in the net were familiar old faces. Former treason trialists Ahmed Kathadra, Nelson Mandela and Walter Sisulu. White Communists Dennis Goldberg and Lionel Bernstein. Harold Wolpe and Arthur Goldreich were not among the eight who were arraigned on charges of sabotage two months later. They escaped abroad. So did Alexander Hepple.

Bruno Mtolo, although a prominent member of the Natal Region of Umkonto we Sizwe, was not in the High Command. Like other small fry he stayed behind to face the music. Special escape plans were only for the privileged and the rich and not for the rank and file. 'We the poor fools were left to nurse their baby', wrote Mtolo in his book *The Road to the Left*.

Documents found at MK headquarters on Lilliesleaf Farm pieced together the activities of these violence-planners. They included reference to the President of the ANC, Albert J. Luthuli, and implied that he gave his blessing to their plot. They listed large sums of money collected and earmarked for the purchase of enough ammunition to start a Vietnam-type confrontation.

Funds came from African states, Communist countries and sources in Britain and the United States. The shopping list included 210,000 hand grenades, 48,000 anti-personnel mines, 1,500 timing devices for bombs and 144 tons of ammonium nitrate. The Soviet Union and Red China paid the band and called the tune. Others joined the chorus without understanding the words.

Directives were clear and concise: 'Shamelessly attack the weak and shamelessly flee from the strong.' But Black attorney Nelson Mandela, the alleged author of a treatise called *How to be a Good Communist*, warned that the ordinary membership should not be informed about this love affair with the Reds.

Well-meaning do-gooders in the United States and Britain were not informed either. How were they to know that their moneys were destined to buy dolls from Red China which contained fuses and detonators and many other tools of terror? How were these responsible citizens in the West to know that Canon Collins's Christian Action was collecting funds for a very unchristian action in South Africa—unchristian both in thought and deed?

A document found on the table at Lilliesleaf Farm near Rivonia outlined the strategy of the MK in detail. Seizing the country by means of sabotage and destruction. Guerilla warfare waged by the masses, supplied with arms and ammunition by Communist and African countries.

'Operation Mayibuye' it was called. 'Mayibuye' is a Zulu word meaning 'Come Back'. The ANC often used the slogan 'Africa Mayibuye'—'Africa Come Back'. Where to? Neatly prepared pamphlets by the underground South African Communist Party gave the answer: 'Higher wages, land, freedom and equality . . . Free bread, free public transport, free education, free medical services, free holidays, free meals at work, no rents . . .' Counsel for the State, Percy Yutar, remarked that free air was about the only thing which the glorious revolution did not promise. Mayibuye, according to Yutar, was aimed at bringing to South Africa 'chaos, disorder and turmoil . . . [through] trained guerilla warfare units . . . [resulting in] confusion, violent insurrection and rebellion, followed, at the appropriate juncture, by an armed invasion of the country by military units of foreign powers'.

Eight of the nine men were found guilty. The ninth, Lionel Bernstein, self-confessed Communist and former treason trialist, was acquitted.

The Rivonia trial was nearing its end. Fully aware of the

spotlight of world attention which focused on the Supreme Court in Pretoria, counsel for the defence decided to call a witness to give evidence 'in mitigation of sentence'. This task was entrusted to Alan Paton, founding member of the moribund Liberal Party.

He described his close association with Albert Luthuli, the self-acclaimed pacifist and Nobel Peace Prize winner, headman of the ANC and spiritual leader of Nelson Mandela, Walter Sisulu, Kathadra and others. The Liberal Party, explained Paton, always operated in close conjunction with the ANC and the Indian Congress. 'I have no doubt whatever of their sincerity, and whatever methods they may have adopted or decided to adopt . . . I have never had any doubts as to their sincerity and very deep devotion to the cause of their people . . . None of these three [Mandela, Mbeki and Sisulu] is known as a person who is obsessed with any desire for vengeance, any kind of racial vengeance . . . '

State attorney Yutar questioned the Liberal author about a television interview which he had with Doug Leiterman of the Canadian CBC network in 1960. 'You visualized bombings and violence,' reminded Yutar, 'and, strangely enough, the ANC went over to the new policy in 1961 ?' Paton : 'You mean there is some connection?' Yutar : 'I am asking you.' Paton : 'There is no connection whatsoever.' Yutar : 'You were just a true prophet?' Paton : 'I would say so.'

A newsman commented : 'Paton went into the box to plead for mercy and found himself on the defensive. He left the witness-box, flushed and obviously angry.' The eight men received life sentences.

There was a tidal wave of indignation from abroad. Even months before the verdict was given the UN Security Council had been approached to intervene on behalf of the accused. The Security Council made strong representations to the South African Government to grant amnesty to all those who had been condemned to death or were 'languishing in dungeons for having opposed apartheid'.

Minister of Justice Vorster, later to become Prime Minister, once again explained that no one had ever been condemned to death or imprisoned because of opposition to apartheid. Opposing Government policy has never been a crime in South Africa, provided, of course, that such opposition does not rely on bomb-throwing or bridge-blowing. He could have saved himself the trouble. These explanations had been ignored in the past. They were ignored now.

In the House of Assembly Prime Minister Verwoerd said: 'We were dealing here with a Communist attack which was discovered not only against South Africa but against the West. These people are criminals, Communist criminals, on the same basis as any spy who has been caught and sentenced to death in the United States; on the same basis as any Communist spy caught in Britain or in any other Western country and sentenced to imprisonment. We are dealing here with a crime against society, based on the Communist struggle against the West.

'Supposing these criminals had succeeded, what type of government would have been established in South Africa? . . . We would have had a Communist-orientated government here . . . and the tyranny which would have arisen would have been similar to the tyranny of the Communist countries . . . Then freedom in South Africa would have been doomed, not only freedom for the minority groups, the Whites and the Coloureds or the Indians, but also freedom for the Black Man of South Africa.'

Mandela and others were the heroes not only of the Communist world, the Afro-Asians, the United Nations and Communist sympathizers in the West. They were also the idols of the liberal press. The *New York Times* felt called upon to remind the South African Government that 'a world-wide campaign of protest has already begun against the life sentences imposed by South Africa's Supreme Court on African Nationalist leader Nelson R. Mandela and seven other foes of apartheid. As the debates and the votes in the United Nations this past year have shown, most of the world regards the convicted men as heroes and freedom fighters.'

'They are considered the George Washingtons and Benjamin Franklins of South Africa, not criminals deserving punishment', proclaimed the *Times*. Protested the *Guardian* from London: 'These men are not scoundrels and eccentrics. Some at least of them are men who would be among the pillars of a just society.' Remarked rank-and-file Black member of Umkonto, Bruno Mtolo: 'I am still afraid to think what could have happened to my own people towards the end of 1963, if the Government had not taken steps in time. As it is, enough suffering was caused to African families through Umkonto we Sizwe.'

In came the letters of protest. From Moscow, New York, London and Peking. From a world seemingly united in its anger over Mandela's failure to destroy Western influence at the southern tip of the African continent and to establish a People's Republic. 'Those cables went straight into the waste-paper basket, because it just does not happen in South Africa that the Government interferes with the Judiciary . . . Our Judiciary is free from all pressure, whether internal or external,' said the South African Prime Minister.

The Leader of the Opposition, Sir De Villiers Graaff, concurred : 'I want to say quite clearly that we of the Opposition want it on record, so that not only this House will know but that the outside world will know too, that we are convinced that the verdicts in that trial were just, that they were necessary and that they were right in view of the actions to which the accused themselves pleaded guilty . . . I want to say that if I have any regret, then my only regret is that they were not charged with high treason.'

Rivonia was a heavy blow to the Communists. But it was not the final one. In Cape Town on 4 July 1964 several young students were arrested in connection with bomb explosions which wrecked power pylons and train signalling systems. Leader Randolph Vigne escaped abroad and left the rank and file members of the Cape branch of the so-called African Resistance Movement to squirm without leadership. So did Bob Watson and Dennis Higgs. As in the case of Umkonto we Sizwe, escape plans were hatched only for the leadership; few, if any, of the lesser members got away. They stayed behind to face severe jail sentences.

Adrian Leftwich, twenty-four-year-old former President of the National Union of South African Students, found another way of escape. A slight man with a shock of brown hair and an aggressive manner, Leftwich became a state witness. Co-operative and obliging, he proved to be damningly accurate in his description of the activities of the ARM which he had helped to establish in Cape Town. He was the ARM's expert on how to withstand police questioning methods, but it took him only a few days to turn against his co-conspirators.

ARM founding father Randolph Vigne had an Oxford education, a charming manner and personality. Coming from a wealthy Kimberley home, the slogan 'Africa for the Africans' sounded strange on his lips. In 1961 he was the unsuccessful candidate of the Liberal Party in the Constantia constituency. This was at the same time his maiden appearance and swan-song in legitimate politics. In 1963 his unorthodox activities earned him a banning order.

Co-founder Bob Watson arrived in Cape Town from Malaya early in 1962, accompanied by an American girl. She was, it transpired, the reason for his departure from Malaya where he was stationed with the British Army. Some of his fellow officers' wives objected to his cohabitation with the girl, considering that he had a wife and children back in London. Watson was never short of money and soon enrolled at the University of Cape Town for a course in African studies. There he met, among others, Adrian Leftwich.

Leftwich at the trial in Cape Town, which both Vigne and Watson skipped so conveniently, explained that Robert Watson instructed the membership of the ARM in the use of explosives. 'He was a former British officer . . .' Interjected Justice Beyers : 'I am glad you did not say . . . and a gentleman.'

These explosives came from clandestine sources in South Africa and from Britain. Among friends in London who collected money to purchase these supplies was former South African John Lang of Christian Action's Defence and Aid Fund. Sent by ship in the false bottom of a crate containing glassware, stored haphazardly in a Cape Town apartment building, transported to targets in ordinary cars and fixed to pylons and masts, these explosives endangered human life every step of the way. Yet the ARM insisted that it never intended to hurt anyone.

Sentencing David Guy de Keller (22), White student, and Edward Joseph Daniels (30), Coloured photographer, Justice Beyers remarked on the absence of Vigne, Watson, Higgs and others : 'Where are most of these now, these men—if one can call them that—that so impressed you? What leaders they would have made in this new South Africa that you were going to build with dynamite !

'. . . These are the people you chose to conspire with to damage your own country. I have not seen all of them. I have seen, and have listened to, that hero of the campus, Adrian Leftwich. Your counsel, in his address, referred to him as a rat. I did not object at the time to that appellation, but on reflection I am not sure that it is not a trifle hard on the *genus rattus*.'

Leftwich removed his spectacles and wept. In another court-room waited Anthony Trew, a twenty-six-year-old clerk, Alan Brooks, a twenty-four-year-old lecturer, and Stephanie Kemp, a twenty-three-year-old physiotherapist, who had pleaded guilty to charges under the Suppression of Communism Act. In Johannesburg and Durban were other cases involving the ARM. The press began speaking of Leftwich as the 'roving witness'. Some months later he was free to go. He left for England, and then proceeded to Canada, but his conscience refused to stay behind.

Friday, 24 July 1964. Only twenty days after the arrest of Leftwich and his young compatriots. Commuters were beginning to crowd the modern concourse of Johannesburg's Central railway station. A chubby young man dressed in a brown overcoat entered shortly after four. He approached a bench where Mrs Ethyl Rhys and her grand-daughter were sitting, left his suitcase at their side and departed.

Soon afterwards the telephone rang in the offices of a Johannesburg newspaper. A man's voice announced : 'At 4.33 a bomb is going to explode on Johannesburg station.' The stunned reporter froze for a few seconds with the silent receiver in his hand, then called the police.

A frantic search started. At 4.33 the timing device in the explosive-filled suitcase short-circuited. Sheets of splintered glass, steel and concrete poured over the milling crowds. Panic-stricken, they fought their way to the exits. Away from the sobbing and shrieking women and children, away from the nauseous smell of explosives, smoke and burning human flesh.

Twenty-three victims were rushed to hospital. Most survived, only to be constantly reminded of that wanton incident by their scars and crippled existence. Mrs Ethyl Rhys died some weeks later. Arrested and found guilty on a charge of murder was twenty-seven-year-old school-teacher Frederick John Harris. The African Resistance Movement chose him for the job, explained Harris proudly. His execution was set for April Fools' Day, 1965.

Pretoria office-bearer of the Liberal Party, Walter Hain and

his family, arranged a petition for clemency. Although supported
from abroad, only three hundred signatures were collected. The
execution went ahead as scheduled. At John Harris's cremation
in Pretoria, fifteen-year-old Peter Hain emerged, lamenting the
death of his good friend and idol. A new radical in the making,
Peter Hain eventually gained prominence in Britain where he
and his unkempt followers disrupted international sports events.

The overseas press hardly shed a tear for the victims of
Harris's wanton act. Instead, there were even attempts to explain
this violent deed as that of a desperate 'mild mannered school-
master' who had 'no other means of expressing opposition' to
the South African Government. Some years later when a similar
bombing incident—involving the Irish Republican Army—
occurred at the Tower of London, the world press found no
difficulty in pinpointing the blame and assessing the true character
of those who were responsible for the killing and maiming of
innocent men, women and children.

Pointing out on 19 July 1974 that one died in hospital and
at least a dozen were injured (about half of them children) in
the London explosion, the *New York Times* commented : 'These
are the enemy against whom the brave terrorists—presumably
of the IRA—who set off the bomb in the Tower of London are
waging their heroic war. These are the civilians whom the fierce
freedom fighters, well hidden and well out of any possible danger
to themselves, are savagely maiming and murdering for the
pleasure of making a political point.' Added the *Times* : 'It makes
no difference what their cause may be. The fanatics who set off
those bombs that injure and kill defenceless innocents are not
heroes, but cowardly criminals.'

It was to prevent other John Harrises from making a political
point by murdering and maiming that the South African authorities introduced the much-disputed ninety-day detention without
trial. Risking further abuse from abroad, the South African
Government knew that there was no other way to contain these
fanatics who set off bombs to injure and kill innocents, while
hiding in safety far away from the scene of the crime. This swift
action by the authorities in South Africa brought violence to an
abrupt end in the mid-sixties.

In Pretoria at yet another sabotage trial Adrian Leftwich was
explaining that the name of the National Committee of

Liberation had been changed to the African Resistance Movement at the suggestion of people in London. These people, he told Mr Justice Bekker, had felt that the name of the organization should be more 'indigenous' and somehow include the word 'African'.

He had been inducted into the movement by fellow student Neville Rubin, a former president of the National Union of South African Students. Leftwich himself was president of this organization in 1960 and 1961. Randolph Vigne, David de Keller and Alan Brookes were active members of NUSAS and the ARM. So were John Harris, the station bomb-planter, and Dennis Brutus, the international *agent provocateur* against sports contact between South Africa and the rest of the world. Bob Hepple, one of the Rivonia plotters and an early escapee, was another former president of NUSAS. Communist Ruth First and her husband Joe Slovo, Rivonia escapees Harold Wolpe and Arthur Goldreich, Robert Watson, Stephanie Kemp and Dennis Higgs of the ARM, Oliver Tambo of the ANC and Lionel Bernstein, an acquitted Communist at the Rivonia sabotage trial—these and many more in subversive South Africa were members of NUSAS.

In a brief spell of eighteen months eighty-seven former students—most of them members of NUSAS—were detained for subversion and sabotage. There was indeed a heavy preponderance of former NUSAS men among the detainees representing the ARM, ANC, Umkonto we Sizwe and the banned Communist Party.

Claiming to represent some 20,000 students out of a total of 60,000 at South African universities on a non-racial basis, NUSAS was formed in 1924. At most English language universities membership of NUSAS is automatic. In 1969 the all-Black South African Students Organization was formed, draining away from NUSAS the few remaining non-Whites who helped to give it a multi-racial appearance.

In the early and middle sixties the NUSAS leadership had good reason to hide its real intent from the ordinary members. In 1964 President Jonty Driver pointed out that NUSAS had two faces—one for public appearances and another somewhat more important one which smiled sympathetically at subversives and saboteurs. In a restricted circular he informed a selected

78

few: 'We have to be very careful indeed that NUSAS statements do not say NUSAS is anti-Communist. It is one thing to say NUSAS is against totalitarianism in all forms; if, however, we say NUSAS is against Communism, we may well run into very grave difficulties both nationally and internationally. . . . ' In that same year Driver was detained under the Suppression of Communism Act and held for twenty-eight days. After his release he quietly left for England where he took up a teaching post.

In recent years NUSAS has continued to run foul of the authorities. Receiving funds from the same International University Exchange Fund in Geneva which finances terrorist organizations like the ANC, PAC and SWAPO (South-West African Peoples Organization) hardly endeared NUSAS to the South African Government. Its friendly connections with a number of openly hostile organizations abroad simply served to stimulate suspicion in South African circles about its real intent. In May 1974 it once again joined with the Anti-Apartheid Movement in Britain and the United Nations in a protest for the 'release of all political prisoners in South Africa'.

Among those whom NUSAS would apparently like to have pardoned is Braam Fischer,[1] now in the tenth year of a life sentence. He was also a prominent member of its fraternity. Leading counsel for the defence in the Rivonia case, Fischer and thirteen others were charged in Johannesburg during 1965 under the Suppression of Communism Act. Eli Weinberg, Jean Middleton, Anne Nicholson, Paul Trewhela, Hymie Brasel and the others were lesser personalities, mostly young, inexperienced party workers. Fischer was the big fish. The master mind behind it all. Top dog in the underground South African Communist Party who pulled the strings in a variety of subversive organizations.

On the witness-stand was Piet Beyleveld, like Fischer a former treason trialist who sat long hours in the old Johannesburg Drill Hall during the late fifties. Also a former President of the Congress of Democrats and one of the Chairmen of the so-called People's Conference which adopted the Freedom Charter, Beyleveld was no small-timer either. In 1961 he was an area

1. Fischer died of cancer on May 8, 1975 after spending some months in hospital and at the home of relatives.

79

committee member of the South African Communist Party. His code name was 'Van' and later 'Rick'.

Mr Berrange (for the defence): 'You must have been a comrade regarded with esteem and trusted?'

Mr Beyleveld : 'I think so.'

From London, which used to be the source of funds for the Communist effort in South Africa, came a meaningful reaction. It came in the form of a newsletter threatening State witness Beyleveld and other 'turncoats' with extinction for the part they played in the dismantling of the Red machine in South Africa. But Beyleveld continued regardless.

'Why?' asked Mr Berrange.

'I recognized that the party had suffered complete defeat.'

Next to take the stand was Secret Agent Q018. Gerard Ludi said he moved in Leftist circles for some time before being asked to join the SA Communist Party. At the first meeting Braam Fischer warned him against the possibility of police infiltration.

'Mr Big' Fischer urged the cell to organize the students of the University of Witwatersrand politically in order to bring about a return to the 'golden days' of the party when Joe Slovo was still at the university.

Q018 described multi-racial parties at which he saw unclothed White married women in compromising positions with non-White men and fights when husbands beat up their wives. He described a party at Fischer's house when the guests plunged into the swimming-bath.

Defence : 'Naked, of course?'

Ludi : 'Of course.'

While he was a reporter on the *Johannesburg Star*, Ludi said, he and the editor had been reprimanded by an officer of the Security Branch for a story he had written about Freedom Radio. This story was used to bolster his standing in the Communist Party. Fischer, he explained, was most indignant and said it was excellent.

'Fischer also said a strange thing. He said it was a shame I had not been locked up for ninety days for the sake of the publicity that would have come out of it. Fischer said newspapermen should try to give 90-day detainees as much publicity as possible. Trewhela, then of the *Rand Daily Mail*, Margaret Smith of the *Sunday Times*, Hazel Fine and I, should do our best to get at least one story a day into the papers advertising the plight of detainees.'

At a Communist Party meeting on 5 July 1963 Fischer spoke for a long time. It was decided to organize demonstrations especially by relatives of detainees—in particular, children—on the lines of 'I want my Daddy'. It was also decided that they should write as many letters as possible to the press and 'pester' the chief magistrate, and try to influence opinion outside the movement, in South Africa and abroad, to protest against the 90-day detention clause.

The next witness was Patrick Baphele, serving a ten-year sentence. He left on the insistence of former treason trialist Leon Levy for training in trade-union practice abroad. Instead, he found himself in China and Russia receiving instructions in the finer art of war. His instructions were clear : return to South Africa and train others to fight the White man.

Then Secret Agent Q034. Slowly but surely the intricate Red spider web was being dismantled and unthreaded. In the middle sat the master spider, Braam Fischer. Restless. When the hearing resumed on 25 January 1965 the thirteen others appeared without their leader. Fischer, QC, had jumped bail and gone into hiding.

'It is the act of a desperate man and the action of a coward,' said senior State Advocate Liebenberg after Counsel for defence read Fischer's parting note which he had found on his desk that very day. A few weeks later five of Fischer's fellow-accused changed their plea and admitted that they belonged to the banned Communist Party. The trial concluded without Fischer. In Cape Town Fred Carneson, former member of the Provincial Council, was sentenced to five years and nine months on charges under the Suppression of Communism Act.

In London ex-British officer Robert Watson, explosives expert of ARM fame who fled the country, spoke to the press. The ARM, he told a reporter, had 'enough explosives and trained saboteurs to have brought South Africa to its knees'. But, explained Watson, 'the South African Freedom Movement as a whole had the attitude that if they made enough fuss and noise the rest of the world would do the job for them. They wanted headlines. They were not equal to the demands of the situation.'

The ANC and its Spear of the Nation, PAC and its POQO,

ARM and all the rest where shattered by an alert and efficient police force. With the broken pieces were large chunks of Alan Paton's Liberal Party membership and NUSAS' 'old boys'. But Fischer was still at large. Braam Fischer, son of a former Orange Free State Judge President – a brilliant barrister who grew in stature abroad as soon as it was discovered that he was not only an Afrikaner but also a Communist! The South African Bar Association, however, was shocked. They had him disrobed *in absentia*. Stories were about that Fischer had fled the country.

In New York a man in clerical robes turned up at UN headquarters. Floating through the well-lit corridors, Canon Collins had a red glow on his face. It could have been excitement—or exasperation. Or both. Canon Collins was quite specific in his address to the UN Committee on Apartheid. Christian Action through its Defence and Aid Fund, he explained, had performed a Herculean task since 1957 in helping subversive South Africa financially. His audience was most sympathetic and lauded this man of the cloth for his fine aid to the disciples of Marx.

On 11 November 1965, ten months after his disappearance, Fischer was rearrested at Corlett Drive in the Bramley suburb of Johannesburg. Rumour has it that his whereabouts were known to the police for some time but that delayed action was preferred so as to enable Fischer, alias Mr Black, to uncover a few more hidden Red threads.

He appeared in court a thinner man with a balder look; experts claimed that he had been depilated to add to his disguise. State witness Bartholomew Hlapane, a former treason trialist and self-confessed member of Fischer's party, related how the accused had dealings with Mandela and the violence plotters at Rivonia.

From a setting of impersonal formality, the story of Braam Fischer reverberated in shock-waves far beyond the dark-panelled walls of the sombre Pretoria court-room. Funds from London. Orders by Fischer to burn maize and sugar fields. Undercover dealings with Red master-minds.

Fischer looked old, far older than his fifty-seven years, when he rose to add the missing pieces to the almost unbelievable jig-saw picture which emerged. He admired decisiveness and he found this in close association with men of violence. He was sentenced to life imprisonment.

From abroad came a stream of protests, challenges and demands. Many from behind the Iron Curtain, others from Western countries. Several written in abusive and uncouth language. Leftist organizations, churches, journalists, artists, women's organizations and professors. A world united in its defence of an arch-Communist who master-minded the planned Red takeover of South Africa by means of violence and bloodshed.

Under the heading PRAY FOR THIS COMMUNIST, Rev. Nelson Gray wrote in the June 1966 issue of *Rally,* an independent clerical magazine in Britain : 'Thank God for such a man and pray for him. If he is a Communist we could do with a lot more like him in the Christian Church.'

The closest affiliation that Fischer had with the Bible in later years was apparently in the despatch of messages to his London contact. Fischer, it transpired, used passages from the Bible as key-words to his codes.

In 1966 also the Prague-based Communist *Information Bulletin* noted sourly that 'the Rivonia trial, the Fischer trial and many other trials, big and small, of the past year have seen many of the finest leaders of the resistance movement sentenced to long years of imprisonment'. Several immediate measures were suggested to combat any feelings of defeatism and despair. 'We call on all South African Communists, whether at home or in exile, to give practical leadership in the fulfilment of these tasks by setting an example of devotion, seriousness of purpose and confidence in the people's victory.'

Early in 1967 Moscow added a footnote. TASS announced that the 1966 Lenin Peace Prize was awarded to Braam Fischer. This award, said chairman Skobelchin, would give this 'outstanding leader of Africa' new strength. It would encourage the fighters against neo-colonialism in the struggle for the freedom of Africa.

Warned *Die Burger*, a Cape Town daily, after the Fischer trial : 'After the series of trials, of which the latest has now ended in a life sentence for the Communist leader in South Africa, the realities of what had been going on in the political underworld under Communist direction are not to be denied any more. It could and did also happen here according to the now-almost-too-well-known patterns of Communist action; it can and will happen again if the security people do not maintain and even intensify their vigilance.'

On 11 January 1965 the 90-day detention clause of the Sabotage Act, which had been the subject of world-wide condemnation, could be suspended. Most of the saboteurs were already tried or in the process of being tried in court.

Enter American Senator Bobby Kennedy as a guest of the National Union of South African Students. The then Junior Senator from New York was invited to speak at the NUSAS Day of Affirmation meeting in Cape Town. He arrived at Jan Smuts airport with a portable record player and recordings of his late President brother's civil rights speeches for Albert Luthuli, a signed copy of *Profiles in Courage* for banned NUSAS president Ian Robertson, lots of PT-boat tie clips and other goodies for street crowds.

*News/Check* magazine reported from Johannesburg: 'With his small athletic figure, his cold blue eyes and famous Kennedy forelock, he was a push-over with university students. Some saw him as the next rung on the ladder to maturity after the Beatles. They mobbed him, they loved him, (sighs of "Isn't he smashing?" from girls) and they listened to him. And if they sometimes didn't catch the lyrics they usually understood the general rhythm—liberty, fraternity and equality.

'The Kennedy visit', added *News/Check*, 'ultimately was no more than a one-night stand in the making of the President 1966/1972 . . . He did not, after all, inject any new ideas in what was often a clichéd and superficial approach. Whether or not he is allowed to make his promised return to the Republic, Kennedy is no substitute for South African leadership. Looking to outside help once again hurt the liberal cause.'

Still in process was a court case in Johannesburg involving three men charged under the Suppression of Communism Act. Said agent John Brooks in evidence: 'Accused David Ernst told me: "Bobby was a big enough clown to focus world attention on South Africa, which was a good thing." '

In Cape Town, nursing a copy of *Profiles in Courage* signed by Jackie Kennedy, Ian Robertson, the NUSAS President, was still under a banning order. Protest marches continued. Questions were asked in Parliament. Justice Minister Vorster explained that he had received a NUSAS delegation which asked him whether he would reconsider the restrictions on Robertson if they could prove to him that the student leader was in fact an anti-Communist.

'I told them that nothing would give me greater pleasure. That was three months ago. To date I have not heard a word from them in this connection and I doubt if I ever will.' Robertson packed his bags and left for England.

In reality that hot December month of 1957 signalled the start of a ten-year period of turmoil in South Africa. The old Johannesburg Drill Hall simply provided a preview of the *dramatis personae*—men and women, many of whom were acquitted, then reappeared on the stage later with their masks off and their torches burning. Cheered on by the world press, the United Nations, governments on both sides of the Iron and Bamboo Curtains, academicians and clergy, they set about burning and destroying with the hope of rebuilding on Communist lines.

Many of these torch-bearers are in jail in South Africa today. Nelson Mandela, Walter Sisulu, Braam Fischer . . . This is the law of the land. Violence and bloodshed are crimes. Many are abroad. Some escaped. Others were allowed out on an exit visa. They are to be found in London, New York, Moscow, Peking, The Hague, and almost every other world capital. Honoured citizens, fund-raisers for the cause, placard carriers, key witnesses at the United Nations—pillars on which the Anti-Apartheid Movement rests. People who, had they practised their nefarious machinations in any other country in the Free World —Britain or the United States or France or Canada—would have been branded as revolutionaries or criminals but who, because it was South Africa's stability and peace they tried to shatter, were lauded as heroes and martyrs.

The internal threat had been averted. But, warned Justice Minister Vorster in 1965, this was not the end. South Africa faced phase four of the take-over attempt. The first three phases were internal. Firstly, incitement; secondly, riots and insurrection, and thirdly, sabotage. The fourth stage, Vorster explained, would be terrorism directed from outside at South Africa's borders. Shortly afterwards the Commissioner of Police, Lieutenant-General J. M. Keevy, announced the capture of eight infiltrators from other parts of Africa.

For ten years and more, terrorists have been active on the borders of Rhodesia and South-West Africa. In Rhodesia South African police were assisting the local authorities because among those who attempt to spread their terror south are members of the ANC and PAC. Once again equipment, training and direction come from the Communist world—in Zambia and Tanzania training camps with Red Chinese instructors make soldiers out of 'recruits', many of them lured abroad from Southern Africa on the pretext of scholarships and university training.

As before, the 'liberal' world had no problem in sorting out heroes and villains. Its idols are in the terrorist training camps —'freedom fighters' who do not hesitate to kill Black and White civilians and to plant deadly mines indiscriminately.

In their appeal for funds abroad these terror gangs purport to be liberation movements bent on freeing an enslaved populace in Southern Africa. They obviously had some success. Not only did the World Council of Churches open its heavenly gates and its coffers for these men of Marx. Even governments made liberal contributions – the Netherlands, Sweden, Norway, West Germany, several American states, Russia and China. A large section of the world press has been sympathetic.

In January 1968 thirty-five terrorists were sentenced to jail in Pretoria under the Terrorism Act. Commented the *New York Times*: '. . . their conviction of "terrorism" under a draconian, retroactive law still remains a travesty of justice and an offense against civilized behaviour.' It sighed with relief at learning that the judge had at least ruled out the death penalty. A few years later, in January 1974, the same newspaper showered praise on a Greek court for acting 'with courage in handing down a sharp and unequivocal judgement' against two Arab terrorists. 'There are disturbing rumors that the Greek Government intends to pardon the two Arabs fully, and expel them from the country', said the *Times*. 'This would only suit the terrorists' purposes: such a hypocritical deal would vitiate the whole Athens proceedings and eliminate the impact of legal punishment as a deterrent to future attacks.'

The inevitable double-standard. In South Africa punishing terrorists is a travesty of justice, while in Athens a harsh judgement for two Arab terrorists is an act of courage and a much-needed deterrent. Equally adept at playing the double game, the

United Nations had no difficulty in condemning terrorism wherever it existed as long as it was not in South Africa. Stirred into commenting on the world-wide problem of terrorism after Lod, Munich, Ulster, London, Rome and a host of other incidents, UN Secretary-General Waldheim called for world action. But in doing so he specifically excluded what he described as 'freedom fighters in Southern Africa'.

As early as November 1970 the *Johannesburg Star* reported on moves in the United Nations to outlaw terrorism. The headline told the story: WHEN DOES A TERRORIST BECOME A GUERILLA? ANSWER: WHEN HE'S ANTI-WHITE. Today these anti-White Communist-inspired 'guerillas' or 'freedom fighters' are seated in the UN as observers. They have come a long way to recognition and respectability considering that the London-based ANC and PAC have as yet not conquered a single inch of land, have not proved to have more than a minute percentage of the support from the Black South Africa which they purport to represent, and have to count their successes largely in terms of civilian deaths and kidnappings.

# 4

# An *Outré* Collection

'What an *outré* collection!' exclaimed a newly arrived South African political *émigré* when confronted in London with a list of his fellow 'exiles'. The journalist who showed him the list also approached several other expatriate activists in the British capital for comments. One pointed in anger to a name, referring to him as 'that —— informer', while another made it quite plain that he was not on speaking terms with others on the list.

An *outré* collection. A mixed bunch. As varied and eccentric as pedestrians in any city street. Once there was complete unity in some odd way. Once in South Africa. Now there were no fuses to burn, no bombs to toss, no violence to applaud. No kicks. Nothing but the humdrum of London's grey streets.

That is where the Anti-Apartheid Movement comes in. Established in 1960, it serves as a soup kitchen for 'battle-weary' arrivals from subversive South Africa. The Higgses, the Hepples, the Goldreichs, the Vignes, the Watsons, the Kemps, and the Leftwiches . . . They all passed through AAM's 'refugee centre' at one time or another to be debriefed and reassigned.

On 4 April 1974 the Johannesburg *Rand Daily Mail* reported that Mr David Davis, a 'banned young trade-union organizer' from Durban, fled from South Africa to Botswana and applied for 'political asylum' in Britain. According to the authorities the bespectacled Davis was a foreign-inspired *agent provocateur* attempting to stir up Black workers. First call when he reached Gaberone in Botswana was to the AAM office in London. Highly placed persons in the Anti-Apartheid Movement, said Davis, had promised to help facilitate his entry into Britain.

When the AAM in London refers to its contact with 'highly placed persons', it is not boasting. Especially in left-wing Labour circles it enjoys good standing. First President of the Anti-Apartheid Movement was Barbara Castle, at one stage Minister of Overseas Development in the Labour Government. Fellow Labour MP David Ennals succeeded her, and after him came Liberal MP David Steel. In 1974 when David Davis made his call to AAM, London, one of the top executives, Joan Lestor, had just been appointed junior Minister in the Labour Government.

In 1963 the Leader of the Labour Party, Harold Wilson, shared a platform at a Trafalgar Square mass rally with individuals who openly advocated violent revolution in South Africa. Organized by the AAM, Wilson used this occasion to pledge an arms embargo against South Africa. Amongst the cheering placard-carriers those with Communist slogans were particularly prominent. Wilson kept his promise when he became Prime Minister. After a brief spell on the opposition benches he regained power in 1974, reintroduced the arms embargo and promised aid to terrorism in southern Africa.

Explained a political scientist : 'The AAM is slightly confusing until you have familiarized yourself with the key names and affiliated organizations. Then it's like playing cards. The same jokers keep showing up. . . .' On the National Committee serve— either as full members or observers—representatives of Christian Action, the Society of Friends, the National Peace Council, the African Bureau, the Movement for Colonial Freedom, the Fabian Commonwealth Bureau, the Liberal Party, the Labour Party and many others. Also represented are a smattering of banned South African groups. The African National Congress, the Pan-Africanist Congress, the SA Indian Congress, the SA Coloured People's Congress and the Congress of Democrats. The National Union of South African Students also has a seat at the AAM table.

These legs of the AAM centipede move in unison on all matters concerning South Africa. It is a versatile creature and feeds on anything as long as it is decidedly anti-Western and left of centre. Commenting on the action of the AAM and its many associates, Harold Soref and Ian Greig noted in 1963 in their well-documented book, *The Puppeteers* :

'It might be asked why no member of these organizations has

ever protested against trade with the Soviet Union, Cuba, Hungary or even Communist China; why the freedom-loving playwrights have not been asked to ban their works being performed in Hungary or Cuba. On the same day it was reported that Mr David Ennals, MP, President of the Anti-Apartheid Movement, who succeeded Mrs Barbara Castle, MP, was attempting to have the export of commercial vehicles to South Africa banned, he was sponsoring a parliamentary pressure group to campaign for a new European alignment to embrace the Soviet bloc as well as the Six and Seven. The prime object of the group is to increase East–West trade.

'Why was there no similar move to prevent the export to Cuba of vehicles which could well be utilized for the transport of troops? Is there any reason for this conspicuous absence of protest regarding the sales of military transport aircraft to Communist China? Have we seen or heard any protests from these people about the dictatorial measures taken in Ghana against members of the Opposition languishing in prision for more than five years?'

Soref and Greig tried to find the answer by tracing the threads of the puppet show backstage. What they found simply substantiated a statement by the former Chairman of the South Africa Society in London, Blyth Thompson, about the AAM and its associates : 'Every single one has a salaried Communist on its management Committee.'

There are those who contend that the Anti-Apartheid Movement itself is a spontaneous product of Britain's indignation over 'racist' South Africa's excesses. Canon L. John Collins disagrees. Had not his Christian Action played midwife and nurtured and nourished the fledgling AAM in 1960? Was not the first home of the AAM the offices of Christian Action's Defence and Aid Fund at 2 Amen Court, London EC4? Canon Collins should know. After all, he and Christian Action have been around on the London protest scene since 1946.

In those immediate post-war years Canon Collins and Christian Action devoted most of their energy and indignation to the Ban-the-Bomb cause. It was only in 1952 that South Africa and apartheid started to feature as targets. What Collins saw as a drift to the left in those early years became a hard core of doctrinaire Communism right smack in the middle of his action group. In the early 1960s Miss Rosalynd Ainslie—her married name is Lanerolli—was appointed to the executive of Christian Action. Holding a job with the East German News Agency in London and being a member of the Communist Party obviously did not prevent her from being an ardent worker at Christian Action.

The 1957 Johannesburg Treason Trial provided Christian Action with a golden opportunity to gain prominence. Thousands of dollars were spent on defence and publicity and the eventful dismissal of the 157 accused was hailed as a major victory for Canon Collins and his group. A letter addressed to Walter Sisulu, one of the Rivonia plotters, in 19 April 1963, by Collins himself, showed that Christian Action's Defence and Aid was not only geared to defence. Informing revolutionary Sisulu that Solly Sachs, a listed South African Communist, was in charge of fundraising for Defence and Aid and that the response 'was growing', Collins added : 'We shall certainly do anything we can to go on helping until the liberation movement succeeds in its purpose.' It's purpose : The murder and rape of South Africa and the rebirth out of the chaos of a People's Republic.

Commented Joel Mervis, editor of the *Sunday Times* in Johannesburg : 'The *Sunday Times*, as everyone in South Africa knows, sharply opposes Dr Verwoerd's policies. But one of the few matters in which we do agree with Dr Verwoerd is that we will not tolerate violence, sabotage and subversion as the means of settling South Africa's problems. When Canon Collins wages a campaign "to support the underground resistance movement in South Africa", therefore, he should not be surprised to find Dr Verwoerd and the *Sunday Times* in the same camp.'

Former South African John Lang, as Director of Christian Action's Defence and Aid Fund in London, lived up to expectations when explosives were required to keep the student members of the African Resistance Movement in Cape Town destructively occupied. Christian Action enjoys wide moral and financial support on both sides of the Iron Curtain. On 25 October 1973 the UN noted with pleasure that 'direct contributions' have been made to Christian Action's Defence and Aid by the Byelorussian Soviet Socialist Republic, the Ukranian Soviet Socialist Republic and the Union of Soviet Socialist Republics.

Miss Ainslie does not have to fight a lone battle against revisionism in Christian Action. Always ready to assist are a bevy of fellow Communists such as Vella Pillay and Abdul Minty, who serve on the executive of the Anti-Apartheid Movement.

'What has happened to Christian Action and its associated clerics and rabble-rousers?' asked the *Durban Sunday Tribune* in 1966. 'Surely they cannot have missed a news item from Leopoldville to the effect that five men, including an army major, have been sentenced to death—which means public hanging—on charges of conspiracy against the Congolese state and being in possession of explosives. Public hanging—could anything be more barbaric?

'Well, now, we are entitled to ask Canon Collins and his boys a few questions. When will the big protest meetings be held in Trafalgar Square? When will the procession of grim-faced MPs take place from the Houses of Parliament through central London? Is the organ playing again in St Paul's Cathedral while hundreds pray for the lives of those under sentence of death? Has Former Archbishop de Blank reserved his seat in the New York-bound jet to see U Thant with yet another petition?'

Said the South African Sunday newspaper rather desperately : 'We would remind Christian Action that the lives at stake are those of Black Africans which, as everyone knows, are more precious than those of White Africans, and especially those of White South Africans. Why then, is no action taken by all those London meddlers in African affairs?'

The answer is obvious. Christian Action, the Anti-Apartheid Movement and all their affiliates are not interested in anything atrocious beyond the borders of Southern Africa. Theirs is a selective indignation—a game of double-standards, played according to Moscow and Peking rules.

This was not the first time that Christian Action had been caught at playing a double-standards game. It was silent before on beatings, murder and mutilation of priests, nuns and missionaries in the Congo, the mass floggings and genocide in Zanzibar, the butchery of 30,000 Tutsis and 600 of Alice Lenshina's Lumpa Church followers in Zambia. And since 1966 it pretended to be blissfully unaware of the killings of tens of thousands of political dissenters in Sudan and Burundi. Even the brutal death of two million blacks in Nigeria failed to stir the 'Christians' into 'Action'.

While ignoring mass killings and blatant cruelty elsewhere, Christian Action has at times even fabricated events to fuel its drive against South Africa. In 1964 Defence and Aid placed an advertisement in the London *Observer* appealing for funds to assist the dependents of people 'prosecuted for their opposition to apartheid'. The case of 'Vuysili Mini and others' was cited as an example. Not explained was the fact that Mini and two others were sentenced for the murder of a co-conspirator who they believed was about to give evidence against them in a court trial.

The *Johannesburg Star,* South Africa's largest opposition daily, was quite shocked : 'Whatever the political overtones, this was a plain case of murder, punishable in this country as in many others with death . . . Defence and Aid and Christian Action may well sympathize with the political objectives; do they condone murder? If so, why not say so? Instead they suppress the fact of murder, make the man a hero. . . .'

In this one instance the advertisement had to be withdrawn. But not without a loud protest from Canon Collins. Since when, he asked, were the British media in the employ of the South African Government? He was obviously not used to being challenged on his fabrications about South Africa. Said the *Johannesburg Star* in rejoinder : 'Defence and Aid's method of raising money, and at the same time rousing feeling against South Africa, was in this case downright dishonest.'

South Africa's reputation abroad was such that people would swallow almost anything, the *Johannesburg Star* complained. The Anti-Apartheid Movement and its fellow travellers are fully aware of this and they tailor their stories accordingly. Playing along are the South African political *émigrés.* There is a definite demand for police-brutality tales, prison stories, torture and starvation. . . . These *émigrés* have no lack of creativity and some have writing talents as well. There's a ready market in the press, among publishers and, for those who prefer live appearances, on TV.

Ronald Segal is a South African exile. When he left South Africa his travelling companions were a South African Communist, Yussuf Daddoo, and compatriot Oliver Tambo, Deputy President-General of the African National Congress. Segal became General Editor of the Penguin African Library in London and advisory editor to the firm's Africa Series. He sees to it that books about South Africa for Penguin's Africa series are without exception written by rabid anti-apartheid men.

Brian Bunting, Ruth First, Patrick van Rensburg and dozens of other South African 'refugees' have received assignments from Penguin in the past few years. In his preparation of an African political dictionary Segal himself found it necessary to call in the assistance of Rosalynde Ainslie, Sonja Bunting and Ruth First.

Sonja Bunting became a Communist when she was eighteen. She came to London with her husband Brian Bunting who served as Chairman of the Cape District Committee of the Communist Party until it was banned in 1950. Ruth First, former acting Secretary of South Africa's Communist Party stepped into London's anti-apartheid society on the arm of her husband Joe Slovo. Joe was largely responsible for the bygone 'golden era' of Communism at Witwatersrand University, when he and Ruth courted on the campus.

Pall Mall Press is also safely in the hands of the anti-apartheid crowd. Ex-South African Colin Legum edits its Africa series. An ubiquitous and uncompromising critic of the White man in Africa, bespectacled Legum enjoys public exposure on television and radio. In his almost Afrikaans-accented voice he found 'East Germany's Herr Guenther Fritsch a young likable immensely able ambassador'. In collaboration with his wife Margaret Roberts, he summed up his wrath against South Africa in a volume entitled, *South Africa: Crisis for the West*—a carefully thought-out plea for punitive action by the United Nations.

Says the jacket blurb of a Penguin book entitled *The Rise of the South African Reich* : 'Brian Bunting is an experienced journalist and a family man.' In the foreword Bunting comes out fighting, a masked Communist masquerading in the name of humanity : 'It is my hope that this book may help to mobilize public opinion in support of the growing campaign to end the most vicious regime the world has known since the death of Hitler.'

From Patrick Duncan, son of a former South African Governor-General, came another book entitled *South Africa's Rule of Violence*. Duncan came to London as a representative of the Pan-African Congress, the tool of terror which crushed dozens of victims in its panga-studded jaws before the police immobilized it. It was of him that Black Chief Minister Kaizer Matanzima of the Transkei said in reference to the callous murder of five people, including two young girls, at Bashee Bridge : 'If it had not been for people like Patrick Duncan, there would have been no killings at the Bashee Bridge.'

Journalist J. D. F. Jones was impressed with Duncan and his views. He wrote : 'It will sicken its readers and rekindle their anger—and some spontaneous anger might be a good thing as the apartheid debate drags on to a stage where we have heard every argument and agreed with every indictment and still do nothing.'

Mobilize public opinion. Sicken the readers. Rekindle their anger. Next came Ruth First with her *South-West Africa*, Govan Mbeki with *People's Revolt*, Albie Sachs with the *Jail Diary of Albie Sachs*. A library of hate literature inundating an unsuspecting naive world. An endless march of books. They also dabble in journalism. Randolph Vigne, former ARM leader, and *émigré* Harold Ruben edit *The New African*, produced in London and banned in South Africa. Like Duncan, Vigne was active in political agitation in the Transkei. Others regularly write contributions for AAM's *Anti-Apartheid News*. Brian Bunting reports for TASS.

In April 1964 the *Irish Independent* introduced the main speaker at the inaugural meeting of the Irish branch of the AAM as being : 'born in South Africa of Irish parents who had to flee the country because of his activities in the Anti-Apartheid Movement'. The *Independent* was writing about Michael Harmel, who shared the platform with Ruth First. Harmel was a member of the Central Committee of the South African Communist Party before it was banned and also Secretary of the Transvaal branch of the Party.

Shortly afterwards Harmel appeared in London at a meeting organized by the 'Marx Memorial Library and Africa Forum'. Ruth First turned actress in a 55-minute special produced by the British Broadcasting Corporation. She called the horrid presentation on television a re-enactment of her experiences in a South African jail. Came the announcer's voice : Miss First 'a housewife and Liberal'. Replied the South African Embassy : But she is a Communist. Came the reply : Is it relevant?

Also on the speaking circuit are Emil and Albie Sachs. Emil

95

Solomon Sachs is a veteran among the *émigrés*. Born in Russia he soon became a member of the South African Communist Party. When he turned up in London after the banning of the Party, Christian Action gave him a job as a fund-raiser. In 1965 his son Albie was detained in South Africa. Solly staged a one-man protest outside South Africa House in London for three months. Albie turned up in London eventually. With him came Stephanie Kemp, convicted member of the explosives set in Cape Town. Lynette van der Riet and Alan Brooks followed. Adrian Leftwich, turncoat leader of the Cape Branch of the African Resistance Movement, showed up in London, then moved on to Canada. He eventually moved back to Exeter University where he runs a programme on Southern Africa.

Also Harold Wolpe and Arthur Goldreich made their bearded presence felt in AAM circles in London. Together with Mandela and others these were the men who plotted the Communist-inspired bloody revolution which culminated in the Rivonia trial. Their lethal weapons in London are placards, and Goldreich's occupation, the designing of houses incorporating apparatus using solar energy for heating. A far cry from the Rivonia days. Later he left for Israel.

Percy and Rica Hodgson are also of South African vintage. They spend most of their time working for the Anti-Apartheid Movement. Hodgson had been a Communist since the Second World War. Wife Rica spoke on Moscow radio in January 1964 : 'The Soviet Union was always a source of inspiration to the people who were fighting for their freedom in South Africa.'

Fanuel Jariretundu Kozonguizi hails from South-West Africa. He has observer status on the executive of the AAM. A most valuable petitioner at the United Nations, Fanuel often shows up in Peking and other spiritual centres. In 1960 he told the world over Radio Peking :

'Our struggle is not isolated. We are struggling for the political and economic independence of our country against imperialism, and the Chinese people, who have already secured political and economic independence and made great achievements, are waging struggles against the menace of imperialism. Therefore the two peoples have a common struggle and we support each other in our struggle.'

Leon Levy came all the way from the Drill Hall in Johannesburg where he sat in the company of more than 150 other treason trialists in 1957. Once in London he was employed on a full-time basis by the AAM. Vallanthum Pillay, a South African Indian and Communist, became Vice-Chairman of the Movement.

Public speaking is hardly a vocation for these men and women. It is an obsession. Sometimes a slip of the tongue occurs. On BBC in 1959 Robert Resha of the ANC said: 'Our aim, *as Communists*, is to gain freedom without bloodshed, but it is difficult to prognosticate what is going to happen in the future.' Later he turned up in North America and New Zealand.[1] A victim of apartheid. A fund-raiser for the good cause. Christian Action and Defence and Aid.

Complained a South African newsman: 'It is an unfortunate fact that the pasts of many of these expatriates are not known to the British public. They are accepted as political refugees who find themselves in London "because we do not agree with the South African Government's policy". They enjoy a favourable press and television interviews are arranged for them. In many cases it is not even known that the people involved are listed Communists who planned a bloodbath in South Africa.'

Membership of the Anti-Apartheid Movement comes cheap. Ordinary individual members pay only a few shillings a year, and student members just half the full rate. Fund-raising campaigns take care of the rest. They are frequent and well publicised by an enthusiastic press and television. A midnight variety concert in London's Prince of Wales Theatre drew a capacity crowd, paying from one to five guineas a head to listen to Eartha Kitt, Cleo Laine and Bernard Braden.

Shakespearian actress Vanessa Redgrave is not unknown in her profession. Vanessa Redgrave topping the singing bill at an anti-apartheid fund-raising concert, with a song composed by herself, is a golden goose. 'I saw a Black man hanging on a tree,

1. In New Zealand Resha was the guest of the National Anti-Apartheid Committee. Challenged about the political hue of its membership, the NAAC's national organizer, Trevor Richards, said in a letter to the Dominion on 19 April 1974: 'I am not aware of the political affiliations of members of our central committee, although I understand that one of two members have been or may still be members of the New Zealand Communist Party. This past or present membership is not a matter which either I, the central committee or the National Anti-Apartheid Committee regard as having any relevance whatsoever.'

Burned by the sun as black as black can be, What can I do to set you free . . . ' The television cameras whirl, the press critics rave and the money rolls in.

'Hatred is the most accessible and comprehensive of all unifying agents', wrote Eric Hoffer in *The True Believer*. 'Common hatred unites the most heterogenous elements'. Carefully nurtured hatred for South Africa is such a unifying agent. It erases boundaries between violence and pacifism, Communism and Christianity, decency and vulgarity, intellect and stupidity. For not all who do their bit for the AAM and its agencies and affiliates are Communists or violent men.

There are also the muddled—easy prey for those calculated Red agents who seem to thrive in the shadows of others. Former Labour MP Fenner Brockway, father of the Movement for Colonial Freedom—one of the pillars on which the AAM house was built—is apparently such a person. Happiness to him meant bringing together twenty thousand people on Trafalgar Square 'on any urgent issue'.

First branding Brockway as a Communist sympathizer, Sir Michael Blundell later corrected himself : 'I recorded that Fenner Brockway was much distressed at this attack, and when I met him and discussed it with him I accepted his assurance that he had no connection with communism. He is a sincere, emotional, rather muddled thinker . . . '

A declaration by the AAM banning performing rights to plays in South Africa solicited signatures from John Osborne, J. B. Priestley, Harold Pinter, Graham Greene, Daphne du Maurier and dozens of others in Britain. From France, Jean-Paul Sartre and from Ireland, James Plunkett and P. J. Bourke. In the United States Arthur Miller and several colleagues signed.

At a black-tie dinner in Washington—AAM went international—participants included conductor Leonard Bernstein, actors Henry Fonda and Van Heflin, Orson Welles and singer Paul Robeson. In Canada a bevy of artists and politicians joined in at the house-warming party of the affiliated Committee of Concern for South Africa.

In The Hague, said a South African newsman, Holland almost seems to have replaced Britain as the nerve centre of the Anti-Apartheid Movement in Europe. A marathon fund-raising programme by the AAM on Dutch television evoked lively and

1. Bonhomie before the storm. The 1961 Commonwealth Conference in London. Left to right: Robert Menzies of Australia, Ayub Khan of Pakistan, John Diefenbaker of Canada and Hendrik Verwoerd of South Africa.

14. World boxing champion Bob Foster on a visit to Johannesburg joins Superintendent Mike Davis on a Highway Patrol.

15. Tennis star Arthur Ashe with a young admirer at Ellis Park, Johannesburg.

sympathetic response. In Sweden and Denmark AAM claims to have seriously injured South Africa's economic interests.

The Anti-Apartheid Movement claims as one of its major achievements a campaign 'which forced South Africa to leave the Commonwealth' in 1961. It often reminds the public that it was at its mass meeting at Trafalgar Square in 1963 that Harold Wilson first promised an arms embargo against South Africa.

It contends that 'as a result of approaches from the Anti-Apartheid Movement, sports teams have refused to tour South Africa under apartheid conditions, and playwrights have refused to allow their plays to be performed before segregated audiences'. It prides itself on being instrumental—with the kind assistance of South African 'exile' Dennis Brutus—in having South Africa barred from the Olympic Games and the International Olympic Committee.

In 1965 Labour MP David Ennals told an AAM gathering at Trafalgar Square that 'all those who attend matches between South Africa and British cricket teams are undermining the struggle'. Dame Laura Knight, composer Benjamin Britten, poet Alexander Trocchi, Baroness Asquith and several others concurred. Messages of support came from UN Secretary-General U Thant, Berlin Mayor Willi Brandt, Martin Luther King and President Nyerere of Tanzania. A few years later Peter Hain and his followers gave direction to the sport boycott move. Several South African rugby and cricket tours to Britain, Australia and New Zealand were cancelled.

Some of the AAM International's claims are obviously inflated, but not all. Often it makes up for a lack of style and depth with versatility and emotional zeal. In one typical period its list of activities read as follows: In Edinburgh where South Africans were scheduled to participate a swimming pool was fouled with dye. In Sweden a Davis Cup match between the home team and South Africa had to be settled in secret in fear of rowdy protesters. At a Lord's game against South Africa heckling placard-carriers tried to block the gate. In Trafalgar Square thousands assembled to commemorate Sharpeville. At South Africa House in London Labour MPs turned up with a wreath for the 'apartheid victims'. In front of Chase Manhattan Bank in New York youths displayed hate placards denouncing financial investment in South Africa.

AAM has failed miserably so far in two major fields of attack against South Africa : trade and investment, and immigration. Pamphlets warning prospective immigrants in Britain against the 'Lush, plush living' in South Africa back-fired. Immigration increased sharply. Early in 1963 the AAM conceived the idea of holding an international conference on sanctions against South Africa. The steering committee in the London conference was headed by Ronald Segal. Two of the members were Communists Pillay and Ainslie. Fifteen of the official delegates came from behind the Iron Curtain. They returned without a working formula.

Lamented Patrick Duncan : 'When a dog has a bone in its mouth it does not bark.' His African proverb was aimed at Britain with her thousand million pounds sterling tied up in lucrative investments in South Africa and her almost irreplaceable trade relations with the Republic.

Nine years later the AAM was still trying to write foreign investments in, and trade with, South Africa out of existence. Co-authored by Ruth First, Christabel Gurney, editor of *Anti-Apartheid News*, and Jonathan Steele of the *Guardian*, *The South African Connection* was counter-productive. It served to remind readers once again of the attractive investment and trade market existing in South Africa instead of actually discouraging them from doing business with that country. Thanked for their kind co-operation in reading and correcting the drafts of this book were Harold Wolpe of Rivonia fame, Vella Pillay and Brian Bunting.

In 1967, when 200 members of Europe's anti-apartheid organizations gathered in Paris for their first hate international, the Chairman of the UN Special Committee on Apartheid was quite despondent. The UN bid to eradicate apartheid had been a failure, said Achkar Marof, the Guinea diplomat who headed the UN Committee at the time. The arms embargo was a 'ghastly farce'. South Africa was still obtaining as many arms as she wanted.

Back to work they went, inflamed with hatred because the object of their hatred seems to grow larger and stronger instead of shrinking with time. Men with a messianic mission. Experts in propaganda. Masters in manipulation of press and television. Back they went to mobilize public opinion in their own areas in support of 'the growing international campaign' to end 'the most vicious regime the world has known since the death of Hitler'.

During a March 1974 press conference, AAM's Honorary Secretary Abdul Minty concluded that the Movement's ten-year-old trade boycott campaign against South Africa had been a failure. He expressed surprise at finding that South Africa's trade relations were expanding by leaps and bounds—despite an ever-increasing support for UN resolutions condemning economic relations with that country. This Communist executive had un-reserved praise for the World Council of Churches, which decided to withdraw its investment from South Africa.

Shortly afterwards Harold Wilson unseated the Conservative Government in a cliff-hanger election and promptly proceeded to reinstate the arms embargo which his predecessor Ted Heath had lifted. All kinds of other punitive measures were announced. But, it was explained, normal trade relations would continue. After all, Britain relies heavily on the South African market. Then came representations from several British trade unions pressing their Government to permit sales of arms to South Africa. The loss of sales, to France, said the President of the Shipbuilders and Repairers' National Association, would lead to redundancies among the already hard-pressed British workers. The AAM has had its set-backs.

A story circulated in Washington at one time that the Central Intelligence Agency backed the American Committee on Africa, co-ordinator of the US anti-apartheid efforts, with generous funds. Another pressure group, the African American Institute, it was alleged, received substantial financial support from the CIA. The idea was that either or both of these organizations, with their well-placed connections among underground and revolutionary circles in South Africa, could serve as useful go-between's 'after take-over'.

The 'take-over' failed to materialize and the CIA found itself sponsoring a charity programme for political exiles instead of a training programme for future leaders in a post-revolutionary South Africa. It is understandably reticent to discuss this abortive excursion into African politics and it hopes that the whole story will die. But the AAI is still around administering favours, financially and otherwise, to a mixed group of ANC and PAC expatriates, as well as to left-inclined White comrades who sought refuge in the United States.

Reported South African journalist Ken Owen from Washington during September 1973 : 'AAI is a tricky outfit. Ostensibly non-political, it claims that it does not "as a rule" take positions on substantive policy questions. South Africa is an exception— AAI is dedicated to ending its White minority rule . . . AAI's President, Mr William Cotter, has testified before congressional committees "in his personal capacity", while taking care to identify himself as president of AAI, and has said he would approve the violent overthrow of the Whites in South Africa if he thought it were feasible.'

Less shy in admitting his violently anti-South African intent and purpose, George Houser of the American Committee on Africa has obtained observer status at UN headquarters. Houser discovered 'racist South Africa' some years ago and found that he could live quite comfortably with a somewhat more explosive race situation on his own doorstep by devoting his energy to violent change in a far-off land. He divides his time between Washington and UN headquarters in New York. In the American capital he is a regular visitor and adviser to black Congressman Charles Diggs whose Black Caucus has helped to keep South Africa in the grime light in past years. In recent years it has sponsored visits to America by terrorist ANC, and PAC leaders.

The ACA has gone academic lately. At Colorado University it runs a 'study center' on Southern Africa, administered by a few Black exiles. Its material shows a remarkable resemblance to anti-South African publications in London, Wellington, Canberra, Paris, Stockholm and the United Nations itself. The same jokers seem to turn up all the time . . . not only in the human resources field but in publications and films. One researcher once discovered that a single lobbyist in Washington served on five different ostensibly independent 'volunteer' organizations devoted to ending apartheid in South Africa. Anti-apartheid has become a major multi-national industry.

Dovetailing with the now defunct University Christian Movement (UCM)—an affiliate of the National Council of Churches in America which was characterized by the *New York Times* as part of the 'new Christian left'—is the Southern Africa Committee. The SAC operates primarily as an information distribution centre, featuring in one single package the monthly *Southern*

*Africa*, church news, terrorist despatches, happenings at the UN and sports. The Churches in the US also have their own thing going—Church Project on US Investments in Southern Africa. Administered by the National Council of Churches its intent is to intimidate investors already active in South Africa and to scare off those who may still want to enter that lucrative market.

In America, as in Britain, South Africa's foes have no problem in cornering the best part of any discussion programme on TV or obtaining reams of column inches in leading liberal journals for their vitriolic messages. The book market is wide open and willing as long as no holds are barred in painting a bleak picture of South Africa. PAC man Nana Mahomo could not help but show open surprise at the celebrity status accorded him when he arrived in New York from London, film in hand. He claimed to have secretly produced *End of a Dialogue,* which portrayed South Africa as a totalitarian state where Blacks live in fear and misery. Mahomo had made it at each of the large TV stations in New York. Reports from London revealing that Mahomo in fact had nothing to do with the production of the film but simply took it over from two White Americans, who moved about freely in South Africa to concoct their phantasmagoric portrayal of that country, hardly made any difference.

Also enjoying preferential status in New York was Joel Carlson of Johannesburg. Billed as a courageous defence counsel for the underprivileged Blacks in South Africa, Carlson was given several opportunities to 'tell his story' in the *New York Times*. This wealthy lawyer played the part of the poor refugee and did it almost convincingly. Nobody was in any case going to believe South African officials who tried to spoil a good story by pointing out that Carlson left rather leisurely and had his wife and children remain back in his spacious mansion in Johannesburg while preparing the way abroad. *No Neutral Ground*, published by Thomas Cromwell Company in New York, tells the Carlson story the way he prefers it—he wrote it himself. He is probably going to write much more as Senior Fellow at the Center for International Studies at New York University.

The anti-apartheid industry has thrown its sparks so far and wide that regular international channels have become necessary to fuel these fires. Foremost among these unifying agents has been the United Nations itself. During the early months of 1974 its Special Committee on Apartheid toured Europe to visit with anti-organizations. In Dublin its arrival was planned to coincide with the tenth anniversary of the Irish Anti-Apartheid Movement, while in London its presence served to bring out the special dinner service and the best tablecloth for a hate feast attended by the many branches and affiliates of AAM.

Another regular international co-ordinator is the Helsinki-based World Peace Council. The oldest and best known of the thinly disguised Communist front organizations, World Peace Council set out from Wroclaw in Poland in 1948 and settled in Finland after being booted out of France and Austria. Serving on its presidential committee are, among others, Oliver Tambo of the African National Congress and M. dos Santos of FRELIMO.

In recent times the World Peace Council has arranged get-togethers in Oslo (April 1973), Moscow (October 1973) and Geneva (January 1974). The Oslo meeting was attended by a band of terrorists and UN and diplomatic representatives—even the Australian Ambassador to Sweden was there. Geared to the violent downfall of the 'regimes in Southern Africa', the Oslo programme required sustained action from all anti-apartheid groups on a co-ordinated basis. In Moscow the WPC had as guests of honour Soviet top brass, including Brezhnev, Kosygin and Gromyko. Russian Secretary Brezhnev received a one-minute standing ovation.

On to Geneva the WPC moved—the implementation of the Oslo Programme again featured prominently on the agenda. And the attendance list? Commented one observer : 'They were all there. The Christians and the Communists, the pacifists and the terrorists, the students and the workers. A complete guide to hate South Africa International.' These were some of them : The Anti-Apartheid Movement in London; Amnesty International; the Christian Peace Conference; Comité Français Contre l'Apartheid; the International Commission of Jurists; the International Union of Students; the International University Exchange Fund; the Afro-Asian Peoples Solidarity Organization; the World Federation of Trade Unions; the United Nations; the World Council of Churches; the ANC; SWAPO and many more. Well might that political *émigré* in London have exclaimed : 'What an *outré* collection !'

# 5

# A Churchy Version of the UN

If the World Council of Churches stopped playing at being a churchy version of the United Nations it could become a better guide to the Christian conscience. This opinion was expressed by the London *Economist* during August 1972. Contrasting the fervour with which the Council condemned 'racialism' in South Africa with its silence on oppression elsewhere, the journal noted that the mass expulsion of Uganda's Asians hardly caused a ripple at the ecumenical gathering in Utrecht, Holland.

'When condemnation of racial discrimination is allowed to be one-sided', declared *The Economist*, 'a body like the WCC is in danger of forgetting its basically religious character.' The editorial concluded: 'It was certainly clear that some of the activists in Utrecht this week knew more about Marx and the revolution than about Jesus and prayer.'

Unusual irreverence in defence of South Africa, coming as it did from one of her own regular critics. But was *The Economist* really speaking in defence of 'the White regime?' Hardly. It was simply an irate, somewhat principled, and usually eloquent, debater airing displeasure at having an illogical stutterer on its side of the apartheid issue. Like the United Nations which it now so closely resembles, the World Council of Churches both in action and inaction has become an embarrassment to some of its best friends in the West.

Like others of the liberal stable—including the London *Times,* and even Malcolm Muggeridge at his acid best—*The Economist's* words had little effect on the WCC. While it admonished, the men of the cloth at Utrecht were plotting yet another assault on the 'White racists' in South Africa—withdrawal of all its capital from companies doing business with these countries. A significant decision, not because of the amount of money involved but for the extent of its one-sidedness. An unofficial estimate puts the sum at $3.7 million. What about companies doing business with all the other 'racist regimes' elsewhere in the world?

Reported Reuters : 'The proceedings were enlivened by a rock-and-dance service led by the Children of Jesus sect. Some delegates joined the long-haired "children" in skipping and stomping around a white-draped altar. Others merely clapped their hands in time to such hymns as "I dig the truth of the Bible, it turns me on".' Paul, it was, who warned the elders in Biblical times that they themselves would distort the truth in order to draw a following.

In WCC circles the name of the late Archbishop William Temple seldom rates a mention these days. Although he served as chairman of the 1938 provisional steering committee to set up a World Council—and wrote extensively on ecumenical matters —his thoughts are buried and forgotten. 'We must be very careful', he once wrote, 'that we do not give the impression that the Church is an agency for supporting Left Wing politics which are often based on presuppositions entirely un-Christian.'

Referring to the practice supported by some 'advanced' churchmen of 'looking round for that proposal in the political field which we think at the moment most likely to help in the right direction', Temple said : 'It is the job of the Christian politician rather than of the Church or its agencies themselves, and there is a great deal of course in the Left Wing movement which is no more Christian than that of the die-hard Right.'

If enough fellow clerics in the World Council had heeded this founding father's sage advice there would have been no rift in the left flank—the Muggeridges and the Carson Blakes, the *Times*men and the Councilmen would still have been in harmony, instead of wasting energy in family squabbles. And churchmen would not have been stomping and skipping around street altars celebrating unadulterated Left Wing war games against some hand-picked White targets in Africa.

A year after the Utrecht happening, in August 1973, the

leader of the Greek Orthodox communities in Britain, Archbishop Athenagoras, circulated a protest letter based on one of his sermons. 'The heart of the WCC has lost its religious pulse and is being overwhelmed by the notions of those who see Christianity as another social movement of history which is not far from economic utilitarianism.' Politics is the concern of the politician, he said, Christians should be concerned with the dissemination of the Gospel. Temple and his thoughts, it seems, have not been forgotten altogether.

In 1948, four years after Temple's death, the World Council of Churches burst on the world scene in a cloud of ecumenical euphoria. This event promised the end, once and for all, of the 'scandal of division' that for centuries had divided Christendom into hundreds of competing and sometimes hostile sects. Some 150 Protestant and Orthodox Churches were represented at this First General Assembly in Amsterdam—twenty-five years later membership exceeded 250 churches in more than eighty countries.

Its initial objective was simply 'to study, witness, serve and advance the common unity'. Geneva became the headquarters. Twelve years later the Council discovered 'race'. In 1960, at the so-called Cottesloe Consultation at Johannesburg, the WCC investigated *in loco* the alleged evils of apartheid. The verdict? Guilty as charged. Shortly afterwards the three Afrikaner Protestant Churches withdrew from the Council. Several other South African Churches remained—including the Methodists, Presbyterians, Anglicans and Congregationalists.

Then came the Third General Assembly in New Delhi, India, during November 1961. Waiting in the wings were a group of bearded clerics from Russia, Rumania, Bulgaria and Poland. Orthodox men, with the Kremlin stamp of approval, who applied for membership of an organization previously decried by the Soviet as 'a façade for Western imperialism'. To ensure a smooth entry for these state-controlled emmissaries, no speeches were allowed in the Council. The ballot was secret.

The Communist bloc was seated on its own terms. Claiming a grossly inflated total membership of 70 million, these Eastern European Churches assured themselves an outsize representation in the assembly and on policy-making committees. While the ecclesiastics at Delhi rejoiced, others made dour predictions. Receiving these churches in the World Council, warned the

Cincinatti *Enquirer,* would only give 'international Communism yet another platform from which to assail the free world'.

To Eugene Carson Blake the seating of the Churches from the Communist world on 20 November 1961 signified a great personal triumph. It was he, this jovial, heavy jowled man, who first established dialogue with the Orthodox Churches behind the Iron Curtain. In 1954 he secured US Government permission to bring a contingent of Czech and Hungarian theologians to Evanston in America for the Council's Second Assembly. At the head of the delegation was Dr Joseph Hromadka of Prague, who returned to his Iron Curtain sanctuary afterwards describing the United States as 'a nation of gangsters'.

But Blake is not a man to be easily discouraged. In almost masochistic fashion he focused next on Boris Dorofyevich Yarushevich (also known as Metropolitan Nikolai). As second ranking prelate of the Russian Orthodox Church, there was hardly anything second-rate about Nikolai's feelings towards the United States. In fact, he specialized in collecting, collating and condemning US 'atrocities' in Korea—such as 'executions without trial and inquisitions secret and public; dreadful tortures of victims—the cutting off of ears and noses and breasts, the putting out of eyes, the breaking of arms and legs, the crucifixion of patriots, the burial alive in communal graves of women with children at their breasts, the scalping of Korean patriots for "souvenirs" . . . ' It was Nikolai who, five years later, ushered in the Russian Orthodox delegation at New Delhi.

Blake's red-letter day marked to many the beginning of the end. Said one dissenter : 'Until now we've boasted that the world dictates the agenda. Now the dictating is being done by the Russians.' Explained William Fletcher, Soviet expert at the University of Kansas : 'The primary objective which Soviet foreign policy hoped to achieve from Russian participation in the World Council of Churches was, of course, to influence its activities in such a way that the Council's decisions and actions would be comfortable to Soviet interests.'

The Soviets succeeded. In 1962, only months after the Eastern bloc Churches were seated, the Cuban missile crisis occurred. Officers of the WCC promptly issued a statement expressing 'grave concern and regret' over the 'unilateral action' of the United States. While condemning in strong terms the

US economic blockade of Castro's Cuba, it had no conscience problems later in demanding boycotts, both governmental and private, against South Africa and Rhodesia.

In 1968, while the free world expressed spontaneous revulsion at the brutal Russian invasion of Czechoslovakia, the WCC remained silent until Soviet goals were achieved. Almost a week afterwards General Secretary Blake issued a tepid and scarcely noticed objection. Ignoring the tens of thousands of persecuted religionists in the Soviet Union—those minority religious groups outside the state approved churches—the WCC found itself so moved by 'those who suffer' in Vietnam that it sent sixteen tons of expensive medical supplies and equipment to the Communist Vietcong insurgents.

Stop the bombing of the dikes in North Vietnam, insisted Blake in July 1972 when President Nixon started a new offensive against the Communist aggressors. At the same time his Council assisted and abetted draft-dodgers and deserters from the American armed forces in Canada and Sweden.

A 'curious selectivity', someone called the WCC's stand on these issues. But no single issue has more clearly exposed the Council's double-standards and selective indignation than South Africa and apartheid. The so-called South African race question became an almost full-time occupation after the seating of the Communists at Delhi in 1961. The leftists and the Marxists called the tune—the rest strung along. In 1966 at a 'World Conference on Church and Society' in Geneva it was decided that the Council should restructure the world into a socialistic Utopia.

Bogged down in the complexities of social, economic and political structuring, chided by the radicals to get going on some clear-cut issue, the conference settled on racism—and South Africa. One of the observers at Geneva described this crossroads event as 'a debate between leftists and extreme leftists'. The Soviets and their bedfellows made the music, while Christianity simply joined the chorus.

Commenting on the Fourth General Assembly at Uppsala in Sweden in 1968, the Rev. Knut Norberg said indignantly: 'Problems related to race, violence and oppression were discussed freely and passionately. But as soon as prevailing conditions behind the Iron Curtain became the order of the day, stony silence reigned.' How, he asked, can an ecclesiastical universal assembly refuse to take notice of the ever-growing appeals from deportation camps, prison cells and torture chambers where fellow Christians are suffering and even dying? 'Is it a matter of tactics? If so, it means total capitulation to the Soviet Union and the Marxist-Leninist religion.'

Says the WCC: 'As Christians we are committed to working for the transformation of society. In the past we have usually done this through quiet efforts at social renewal, working through established institutions. Today, a significant number of those who are dedicated to the service of Christ and their neighbours assume a more revolutionary position.'

With this mandate the WCC's so-called Programme to Combat Racism was launched—headed by a hawkish Hollander, Baldwin Sjollema. In May 1969 Sjollema's 'committee on race' sponsored a 'consultation' in Notting Hill, London. Chairman on that occasion : Senator George McGovern, who later became a landslide loser in the race for the Presidency of the United States. The participants included several Black Power militants from America.

Bolstered by rare successes in the United States where many churches cowered when they threatened, these Black Americans were quite immodest in their demands. A Black identified as George Black demanded millions of dollars from White churches in reparations for the ills done to his people. He needed twelve million dollars to defend Huey Newton, Eldridge Cleaver, H. Rap Brown and other Black Panther luminaries; seventy-seven million to support various 'liberation movements' and forty-eight million to establish a propaganda publishing house dedicated to Malcolm X and Che Guevara.

All this blackmail was taken quite seriously. The delegates, after a lengthy discussion, supported the principle of reparations. But America was hardly a priority. South Africa was. And the 'race committee' reserved its strongest recommendation for that part of the globe : Economic boycotts against corporations and institutions doing business in racist South Africa and, 'all else failing', support for 'resistance movements, including revolutions'.

In September 1970 the specifics of this revolutionary programme became known after it was approved by the 120 member Central Committee. The American Blacks hardly featured at all—Asian and African delegates felt these 'well-off' Negroes could look after themselves. Instead, the WCC utilized 200,000 dollars in Council reserve funds, opening a special account to assist nineteen terrorist movements. Most of these operate actively against South Africa, bent on destroying and killing and maiming regardless of race, colour or creed. The old hands in the WCC blinked in disbelief. Four of the most generously financed groups were avowedly pro-Communist, receiving their arms, training and direction from the Soviet Union and Red China.

They were all there—the Pan Africanist Congress (PAC), the African National Congress (ANC), the South-West African Peoples Organization (SWAPO) . . . agents for Marx and Lenin suddenly enveloped in a shroud of Christian respectability. Conspicuously absent from this largesse list were those insurgents fighting against Communism elsewhere in the globe.

The press pundits—among them fierce critics of the South African scene—were themselves surprised and even shocked to learn about this fiery cross approach. The London *Times* contended that 'Christian authorities have no business to support organizations avowedly engaged in the use of terror, whatever their grievances.' Said the London *Daily Telegraph* under the heading HOLY TERROR: 'Once it was missionaries who received our funds for their dispensaries and schools. Now it is obscure, many-lettered organizations which plant explosives by night and are enemies, conscious or unconscious, of all peace and prosperity.'

Germany's *Die Welt* commented flatly: 'Christian faith and terrorist power are incompatible.' Also Malcolm Muggeridge, one of Britain's foremost liberal commentators, objected strongly to the association of the name of Christ with these terrorist groups in Africa. Although he, as one of South Africa's most persistent critics found their cause 'laudable', he failed to see what such upheavals had to do with advancing the Kingdom of Christ— 'presumably the essential purpose of the World Council of Churches'. 'Is Kenya more Christ-like because Jomo Kenyatta now rules over it?' Muggeridge asked. 'Or the Congo because President Mobutu is in charge? Chuck it, World Council of Churches!'

The WCC did not chuck it. Instead it set out to justify its decision—one that was rammed through by the 120 member Central Committee in spite of the WCC constitution which precludes it from taking action other than that specifically requested by the full membership. The Director of the so-called Programme to Combat Racism, Dutch sociologist Sjollema, announced that assurances were given by the 'liberation movements' in Southern Africa that the World Council's money would not be used for military purposes.

'They have given the assurance that the funds will be used for their social welfare, health, educational and legal aid programmes,' he contended. 'There is every reason to trust the assurances given by those movements, he said—and then reluctantly admitted : 'Of course, there are risks involved in the decision.' Wilbur Forker, another functionary of the Council, came to Sjollema's rescue : 'The money will definitely not be used for arms. We have assurances in writing from all the groups.' Then the Council's Director of Communications argued that although the money was intended for terrorist groups' welfare and not warfare, 'these two aspects may sometimes overlap'. And finally Sjollema himself conceded : 'Grants are made without control of the manner in which they are spent.'

The South African opposition daily, the *Natal Mercury*, commented : 'After voting 200,000 US dollars to guerilla groups in Southern Africa and anti-apartheid factions in Britain and elsewhere, the executive committee [of the WCC] "noted with appreciation" that the groups had given assurances that the money would not be used for military purposes, and comforted itself with the thought that the United Nations would control the spending of the grants . . . What in God's name, does the Committee think a guerilla group is if it is not wholly military in concept, purpose and operation? And not military in a conventional sense, but dedicated to intimidation and terrorism among innocent civilian populations by murder, arson, torture and rape.'

It was obvious that the World Council of Churches had no control over the way its donations were spent. Nobody puts a leg of lamb in a tiger's cage and expects him to hold it for a week before he starts nibbling at it. But the WCC had to pretend. And it had to at least make an attempt at underplaying the real nature of these terrorist movements. For example, eighteen months later, shortly before his retirement as WCC General Secretary, Eugene Carson Blake told the press : 'People have charged us with supporting rapists or terrorists . . . As for the fact that some of these liberation groups might be Communist, I don't know, but we have not lost a member church by granting these funds.'

Seriously contemplating resigning in protest against the WCC's aid-to-terrorism decision, even English-language South African Churches eventually decided to stay on. (The Afrikaans Protestant Churches had, of course, walked out years before following the Cottesloe 'consultation on race'.) South African Prime Minister John Vorster was not pleased with this violent transformation of the WCC. He showed his displeasure by preventing any of these remaining South African member churches from sending funds to the World Council's Geneva headquarters. To him and South Africa it made sense to prevent funds from your own country being used in one way or another to equip the enemy. Yet, there were those in local church circles who complained of Government interference.

Blake's was not an inflated claim. He not only managed to keep all the sheep together after Notting Hill, he even managed to expand the flock. Gathering sheep and keeping them together, however, is one thing. Fleecing them is another. At the very next opportunity—Addis Ababa, January 1971—the Central Committee launched a new appeal for more contributions to its murder fund. The reaction of those who could afford this brutal luxury was lukewarm, while the enthusiasts in Africa, Asia and the Communist world found themselves slightly out of pocket.

Henry Reuter reported from Addis: 'Although the WCC executive committee worked hard to paint a different picture, all the ginger of the debating lay in the racism issue. Fresh faced American Baptists, bearded Coptic and Orthodox patriarchs, pompous British bishops and the *avant garde* of the established church, a team of "youth advisers" whose dress was sometimes as flowery as their prose, all "did their own thing" to help shift the Black man's burden. Several speakers reiterated that the WCC's special fund to combat racism, of which part had already been allocated to "liberation organizations", was aimed at White racism in particular. By this, it became apparent, was meant the oppression of Blacks by Whites.'

There were tentative cries of 'but what about Moscow-generated suppression of the Church in Czechoslovakia and elsewhere'. These were quickly glossed over. Observers gained the impression that idealism didn't go that far. Outside the conference hall a Southern Sudan Liberation Movement deputation pleaded with the World Council's big-wigs for assistance against their oppressors. They were told: 'Our main preoccupation is with fighting White oppression.'

Later the Sudanese fighters were informed that their case had been considered and that they might very well be allocated a small sum in the next WCC war budget. But, they were told, the Sudanese Ambassador in Addis Ababa had been consulted with a view to channelling the aid through official sources. One member of the deputation commented wryly : 'It's like channelling funds for the Southern African terrorist movements through the Vorster Government. They'll never get it.' This was the abortive end of the Sudanese oppressed people's encounter with WCC morality—a people who averaged 100,000 deaths a year at the hands of their rulers.

The WCC appealed for close on half a million dollars to wage their anti-White war. They found some people quite tight-fisted. Commented Reuter : 'Surprisingly it was American and British church leaders who led opposition to the special fund support for violent organizations. Motives varied. Quakers and Lutherans expressed abhorrence at all violence. Methodists wriggled unhappily. And a Baptist spokesman, Dr D. S. Russell of Great Britain, raised visions of old ladies who starved their canaries all week to put their pennies in the collection boxes throwing up their hands in horror when they heard of the uses to which the pennies were being put.'

Eugene Carson Blake was not to be dissuaded that easily. Visions of little old ladies starving canaries or pacifist priests within his ranks notwithstanding, Blake reminded the world that donations to the terrorist fund were hardly enough. There were new and important targets ahead—for instance, Cabora Bassa. Constructed by a consortium of southern African nations with South Africa as the major partner, Cabora Bassa is generally recognized as one of the more important projects to be tackled in Africa. Bigger than all other dam projects on the continent, the enormous wall spanning the mighty Zambezi River at Cabora Bassa in Mozambique could mean wealth and progress to half a dozen Black and White nations.

Blake saw in Cabora Bassa White racism symbolized and was

in no mood to weigh its advantages to both Black and White in Africa. Reports at the time of a 300-strong terrorist task force being trained by the Communists in Tanzania to destroy the rapidly rising concrete wall at Cabora must have pleased the WCC's General Secretary. After all in a way these were his troops. Unfortunately for Blake and the Communist instructors, the Portuguese were equally intrigued by this venture. Acting on intelligence reports, they flew paratroopers into the Tete area in good time. More than seventy terrorists died; the rest left in a disorderly fashion, leaving a trail strewn with an assortment of Russian and Chinese weapons and ammunition.

Kunene, another large-scale hydro project spanning the width of the river bordering Angola and South-West Africa, did not escape attention either. Director Sjollema of the Council's Programme to Combat Racism, expressed satisfaction at a WCC-sponsored terrorist organization's expressed aim to destroy the dam. Less happy, however, about moves to improve the wages of Blacks in South Africa, Sjollema explained his odd stand to a bevy of surprised newsmen in London. This campaign in the British press and House of Commons for higher wages for Blacks in South Africa was 'not helping the situation', he contended. It was 'dangerous'. Improving the Black man's standard of life in South Africa, he argued, would narrow the scope for agitation and so inhibit radical change !

Commented Alexander Steward, a prominent radio journalist in South Africa : 'What could reveal more starkly the real nature of the professed humanitarianism of South Africa's opponents? It is nothing but a cloak for the sowing of disorder and anarchy —because what, in straight language, Dr Sjollema is recommending is a suppression of the Black people which will drive them to revolt and violence. The end must be achieved, not by orderly reform, but by the desperation which grows from the imposition upon a people (engineered if possible by the WCC) of deprivation and misery.'

South Africans who knew something of their country's history may have been tempted to compare Sjollema with witch-doctor Umlakaza, who in British colonial days imposed upon his own Xhosa people deprivation and misery—and in doing so tried to engineer a major war. It was in 1857 that Umlakaza's buxom young niece Nonkwazi emerged from an evening of solitude to bring strange tidings of ancestral ghosts demanding that this Black nation destroy all their cattle and crops. Everyone, said Nonkwazi, should wait for 12 February, when a whirlwind from the east would blow every White soul into the sea and fill the land with cattle and crops again. Her uncle, Umlakaza, was father to the plot.

The Xhosa obeyed. On the day of destiny they gathered and waited. In vain. Then, instead of plundering and fighting the White 'intruders' as Umlakaza expected them to do, they stumbled on to White-owned farms begging for food. Many were saved from starvation. Thousands perished. Sjollema, the latter-day witch-doctor, should take note. Deprivation and misery do not necessarily lead to successful uprising. Calling for the economic suppression of Blacks in South Africa does not automatically guarantee revolutionary success.

Eugene Carson Blake has retired now. There is a new man in his office at Geneva with that picturesque distant view of Mont Blanc. Dr Philip Potter is a West Indian—he claims his ancestry includes strains of Irish and African slave. The *Guardian* noted that the new General Secretary had brought calypso to the 1973 Geneva gathering of the WCC—'a pleasant distraction from Christendom'. The other distractions—terrorism and war games —Potter hardly introduced. He simply took over where Blake left off.

Potter showed no hesitation when questioned on British television about his future strategy in Southern Africa. Pontificating about love, justice and peace, he concluded : 'I am prepared to face chaos and anarchy if that is what it takes to bring about the necessary change in the world.' The war was still on and terrorism found a new promoter at WCC headquarters in Geneva.

In that same month several Blacks were killed in Rhodesia in murder orgies arranged by terrorists to intimidate the un-cooperative peace-loving populace. Then followed an abortive kidnapping attempt at a Black mission school in order to Shanghai teenage trainees for terrorism. The war was on indeed. General-Secretary Potter was interviewed by the *Guardian*. 'I find that the more one is rooted in Christ, the more radical one is,' he said.

It's a concept which does not please all, admitted the *Guardian*.

It seemed to please the Communist-guided terrorists in Southern Africa. It may even have pleased others at Munich and Lod Airport if it were also directed at them. But formal WCC support for terrorism was reserved for Southern Africa.

A South African newspaper carried a cartoon illustrating this selective violence on the part of the World Council of Churches. It showed two priests leaving the WCC conference hall at Utrecht passing a poster announcing the tragic killing in Munich of Israeli athletes. One priest says to the other: 'Fortunately they are not ours.'

At Utrecht in 1972 the WCC doubled the funds for its Programme to Combat Racism. A year later there were attempts once again in Geneva to broaden the scope of this programme. These failed miserably. When Eastern Europe was cited together with South Africa as an area where there were oppressive social and political structures, Orthodox churchmen from the Communist world intervened. The paragraph pertaining to oppression behind the Iron Curtain was deleted, to the surprise and dismay of the few who tried to be even-handed in the fight against racism. At the same meeting 650 companies doing business with South Africa were black-listed.

Like owner and dog, the United Nations and the World Council of Churches were beginning to resemble each other in looks and habits. Strolling down Kill-White-Southern-Africa-Street it's difficult to know who is leading whom, because sometimes the dog is ahead and sometimes the man. The Third World is providing the votes and the Communists are calling the shots. The West is simply paying the bills. Both adept at the double-standard game, Black Africa and the Communists find no problem in isolating mutually acceptable targets, exchanging expert advice and acting in concert.

In Africa the WCC established a formal link with the militant Organization of African Unity and launched Africa 2000. A new anti-apartheid movement, Africa 2000 operates from a gloomy office in Lusaka, stocked with shelves of anti-South African books and posters carrying photographs of Che Guevara and other revolutionaries. The United Nations has been in the anti-apartheid propaganda business for many years and has devoted a disproportionate share of its publishing funds to the writings of Communist and other critics of White Southern

Africa. These books and authors it now often shares with the WCC.

Lukas Mangope, Black leader of the South African homeland of Bophuthatswana, grouped the UN and the WCC together in an attack on what he termed their 'complicity in the murder of the innocent'. Condemning support of terrorism at both these organizations Mangope said : 'They who know nothing of our conditions and problems in this country have individually and collectively in world councils arrogated the right to judge, to condemn and to appear unasked as the champions of the oppressed peoples of Southern Africa. Do they regard us, their Black brethren, as they like to call us, as too immature, too stupid, too cowardly to fight our own battles?'

The answer to Mangope's question is obvious. His well-being and that of his fellow Blacks in Southern Africa is of little consequence or importance to these advocates of violence in the UN and the WCC. What is important is the final goal : A Southern Africa ruled by a Government willing to forsake Western principles in exchange for Communism—another piece in the Red world's composite for future global happiness.

At its next Assembly in Jakarta, Indonesia, in 1975 the World Council of Churches is expecting 3,000 people, including 800 voting delegates from 267 member churches in 90 countries. The theme will be 'Jesus Christ Frees and Unites' and will allow for 'theological research into the multi-faceted nature of violence'. Further steps against Southern Africa are expected, more support for violence in that part of the world—and further consolidation of the Council as an instrument for radicalism and socialism and Communism.

In July 1972 the England-based *Intelligence Digest* observed that 'the WCC may be a powerful body and the "Geneva Curia" may rule millions of still-believers, but their social gospel and perversion of the Christian faith has opened more and more eyes amongst those who see the real danger of this "ecumenical" movement, in America and Europe as well as in Southern Africa'. It added : 'As a matter of fact, ethical and liberal pastors preaching hatred and turbulence instead of the Grace of God and the love of Christ find a growing number of churches becoming empty.'

At about the same time American author Dean M. Kelly

published a sociological study entitled *Why Conservative Churches are Growing*. In it he contended that religious people in the United States were tired of anti-Western propaganda from the pulpit. They prefer the real gospel they were used to listening to and they leave the corrupted clergy alone, Kelly opined. In the past few years there was in fact a pocket-book rebellion of sorts among more conservative churchgoers in the US and other countries. The Federation of Swiss Protestant Churches expressed dismay at discovering that the WCC was being administered by a permanent staff of functionaries who 'have lost all meaningful contact with church life'. In Lausanne during July 1974 world evengelical leaders were seriously considering the possibility of establishing a new world church organization as a rival to the World Council of Churches. Most of the 2,700 assembled at Lake Geneva felt the WCC neglected basic human spiritual needs and became too involved in political and social issues.

Still, this grass-root rebellion against church involvement in politics and Marxist-inspired bloody revolutions has not deterred the WCC command. In 1974 it launched an active harassment campaign against overseas financial institutions involved in Southern Africa and made yet another donation to terrorism—the largest ever.

# 6

# Et Tu Brutus?

Munich Olympic Stadium. Sunday, 24 June 1973. The spectators, a mere shadow of the capacity crowds during the 1972 Olympics, cheered enthusiastically as the contestants in the 1,000-metre event sprinted past the finishing line. A fitting conconclusion to a remarkable record-shattering race in soggy weather.

Celebrating his twenty-third birthday, South African athlete Daniel Malan finished first—ten metres ahead of the field and two-tenths of a second inside the eight-year-old world record held by Juergen May of East Germany. 'Joseph was magnificent,' Malan said afterwards. He was referring to Joseph Leserwane, his Black fellow South African. Leserwane's mission it was to set the pace.

The Johannesburg *Rand Daily Mail* reported from Munich: 'The partnership was indeed magnificent. Leserwane took the initiative from the gun, streaking ahead of the field. Malan tucked in behind him, jostling with the field of eight international-class German runners. . . . At about 500 metres Malan suddenly broke from the crowd and signalled Leserwane to open up. The beautifully muscled African did so with a classic sprint, towing Malan behind in the now pelting rain. . . . The two South Africans went though the 600-metre mark in 85 seconds, still behind schedule. At the 650-mark, Leserwane finally blew up and dropped out of the race as Malan tore past him.'

Both Malan and Leserwane were barred from the 1972 Olympics in Munich. So was March (the Hare) Fiasconaro, who smashed the world 800-metre record in Rome barely two weeks after the Leserwane–Malan triumph. At one stage it was argued that Fiasconaro, an Italian-born immigrant to South Africa, would be accepted at the Olympics as a member of the Italian contingent. In the end he did not go.

World-class athletes, swimmers, boxers, weight-lifters and canoeists were all barred from setting foot at Munich during 1972 if they happened to come from South Africa. This ban applied to all alike—White and Black. For twelve years now, since the Tokyo Olympics, this has been the case. And in the process hundreds of deserving sportsmen have been robbed of the opportunity to compete for the world's most coveted awards.

In Amsterdam on Friday, 15 May 1970, South Africa was finally expelled from the International Olympic Committee. In the official jargon of the Committee there was a vote of 35 to 28 to 'withdraw recognition' of South Africa. The 'charge sheet' was drawn up by the Supreme Council for Sport in Africa. South Africa stood accused of racial discrimination in sport and failing to provide adequate facilities for Black athletes.

The same Supreme Council for Sport in Africa which acted as accuser, prosecutor and judge in Amsterdam, finds itself on rather slippery ground when it condemns others as being racist. As the handmaiden of the Organization for African Unity, this 'sport council' subscribes to its ideals and principles. Stated the OAU: 'We cannot compromise with any White government, extreme or liberal—or agree to multi-racial nonsense. We are determined to destroy all the vestiges of White civilization. The rivers are to run red with the blood of Whites and their children.'

South Africa was ousted from the IOC by Africa's Supreme Council for Sport because it allegedly practised racial discrimination in sport. The Communist countries threw in their weight behind this ouster—and several Western countries followed suit. Metaphorically speaking it was a question of the church choir being led by the town harlot—and no one daring to protest for fear of being roughed up by the local Mafia.

Representing such models of tolerance and integration as Uganda, the Supreme Council for Sport in Africa felt called upon to have its President Ordia express the sincere hope that 'now there may be some changes of policy in South Africa'. Thousands of displaced Indian refugees from Uganda and Kenya and the surviving relatives of thousands killed in Nigeria, Sudan and other newly independent Black states may have found this statement by Ordia odd, to say the least.

Nevertheless, there was even among those Western nations which displayed the courage to object to this ouster a sigh of relief. The ransom was paid and the world sat poised for a great event in Munich. With South Africa out of the way there was no reason why the 1972 Olympics should not take place in the best tradition of Pierre de Coubertin. Such were also the hopes when South Africa was barred from Mexico City in 1968, the pessimists recalled. But that event was marred by student riots and ugly manifestations of race hatred on the part of Black Power adherents in the American team, despite South Africa's absence.

Munich was doomed right from the outset. With South Africa already excluded, the Supreme Council for Sport in Africa focused its jaundiced eye on an integrated contingent of Rhodesian athletes. Unless the Rhodesians were told to leave, they declared, Black Africa would excuse herself. Several Black American athletes joined the blackmail bandwagon and once again the organizers obliged. Rhodesia was barred 'to save the games' and in the process fourteen Black Rhodesian athletes also lost their chance to compete.

James Coote of the *Daily Telegraph* was there. This is how he described the IOC's rationale : 'By the time the Supreme Council for Sport in Africa and the Organization for African Unity had made their threats of boycott (should Rhodesia be allowed to participate), the IOC had no alternative but to take a vote and the vote by narrow margin was that Rhodesia should leave—a decision which proved that this committee was as susceptible to verbal blackmail as other mortals.

'They feared that if they voted to allow Rhodesia to compete, many countries, some no more than dots on the world atlas, but whose presence is felt in the sporting arena, might indeed carry through their threats and pack up and go home. Instead it had to be Rhodesia's athletes, Black and White, that were obliged to go home.' In essence, therefore, the same argument and blackmail tactics which applied when South Africa was black-balled.

While the International Olympic Committee was undergoing cosmetic surgery by expelling South Africa and Rhodesia to satisfy its scar-faced suitors—the Supreme Council for Sport in

Africa and its militant supporters in the Communist world and America—a malignant growth went undetected. On Tuesday, 5 September, it broke into the open. The news flashed to a shocked world that nine Israeli athletes were being held hostage in their second-floor quarters in the Olympic village by a group of Arab terrorists.

The Black September gang demanded as ransom the release of some two hundred Palestinian terrorist prisoners in Israel. For the whole day—with the Games suspended—bargaining continued. The West German Chancellor, Herr Willy Brandt, personally tried to intervene, to no avail. The day ended with eleven Israelis murdered in cold blood and several terrorists gunned down by German police at a nearby military airport.

The next morning the Olympic Stadium became the scene of a moving memorial service. On the field Munich's famous symphony orchestra assembled to perform Beethoven's Funeral March. The eighty-four-year-old outgoing president of the IOC, Avery Brundage, spoke pointedly of the double intrusion of politics that ended in such tragedy—in the sorrow of the moment he could remember only Rhodesia and Israel and forgot about the third, South Africa.

West Germany spent close to two billion dollars to make the XXth Olympiad in Munich the best ever. The IOC assisted by giving in to the ransom demands of Black Africa and their Communist friends. By booting out Rhodesia and South Africa, the IOC hoped to save the event. Yet, as tens of thousands of spectators and competitors left for home, there was, despite some remarkable athletic feats, little room for rejoicing. 'A fairground in a graveyard' is how one commentator described Munich's Olympic town in those closing days.

Politics in sport is not Black Africa's invention. Right from the beginning when Baron Pierre de Coubertin staged his first modern Olympics in Athens, political incidents occurred. In 1920, just after the First World War, Germany and Austria were not invited to the Games. In 1948 the vanquished Axis powers were snubbed again. In 1936 some countries threatened to boycott the Berlin Olympiad in view of Hitler's crude exploitation of the event and his discrimination against Jews and Negroes. In 1948 the IOC ruled that the new state of Israel could not participate because it was not yet a member. This decision averted a threatened walk-out by the Arab states. In 1956 Red China withdrew from the Melbourne Games when the flag of National-ist China was run up in the Olympic village.

At the 1952 Olympics in Helsinki there were several Western countries which threatened withdrawal if the Communist bloc countries were invited—they reneged eventually. Four years later, however, Spain, the Netherlands and Switzerland with-drew from the Olympiad in Melbourne in protest against Russia's savage quelling of the Hungarian uprising. Egypt, the Lebanon and Iraq were also absent, walking out in protest against the Israeli attack on Egypt and the British and French occupation of the Suez Canal area.[1]

In 1956, some years before the campaign against South Africa commenced, President Avery Brundage complained : 'In ancient days nations stopped wars to compete in the Games. Nowadays we stop the Olympics to continue our wars.' But all these political happenings which preceded the big offensive against South Africa were singular events and never seriously threatened the membership of any participating nation. It was Black Africa, with the brotherly help of the Communist world, which showed the way towards complete politicizing of the Olympic Movement. The same humourless dedication which characterizes their onslaughts against South Africa in the United Nations typified their actions in the area of sport—and led to the final expulsion of this founding member of the IOC.

In 1908 South Africa became a member of the International Olympic Committee. That same year she won her first gold medal in the London Olympiad when Reginald Walker streaked across the finishing line in the 100 metres, ahead of James Rector of the United States and Robert Kerr of Canada. Four years later, in Stockholm, South Africa's Kenneth McArthur and Christopher Gitsham finished first and second in a gruelling marathon race. Until 1960, when she last participated in the Olympics, this had been the pattern for South Africa : At least a gold medal or two, perhaps three, and a few silver and bronze ones at every meet. Modest when compared with modern-day

1. At the 1974 Asian Games in Teheran Israel was once again a political target with Red China refusing to meet Jewish athletes in head-on competi-tion such as fencing and tennis. The Chinese had no qualms, however, about competing against the Israelis 'in races against the clock.'!

Russia or the United States, but more than merely respectable when compared with her peers.

Abundant sunshine and mild winters make South Africa an outdoorsman's paradise. Growing up as they do in a country where separate development had always been a way of life, it was hardly strange to find in 1955 that White and Black each utilized their respective share of this abundant outdoor commodity separately. After all, in the United States, where integration has long been declared policy, the Negro only started really to break into 'white sports' during the post-war years. Describing conditions reigning in the United States when Jesse Owens was at the height of his career, immediately before the outbreak of the war, Richard Mandell wrote in *The Nazi Olympics*:

'Negro athletes who were winning sometimes had to defend themselves against interference on the part of resentful spectators. . . . When the Negro amateur boxer travelled with his team, local mores in the United States usually required that he eat apart from his mates and, if he was allowed to use the same hotel as they, to use the back entrance established for cleaning women and garbage men. There were, of course, no Negroes on any major league baseball team. . . . The happy situation described above existed in the enlightened far North. Things were worse in the South.'

The Negro in America rapidly achieved stardom in a dozen or so athletic pursuits—including baseball, basketball, football, athletics and boxing. Despite Ashe, the Black American's efforts to corner the tennis industry have been relatively unimpressive, while he is almost totally absent in wrestling, yachting, archery, long-distance running, swimming and a number of other sports. Some explain this absence in terms of physical adaptability—others feel that lack of finances may have something to do with it, especially in yachting, tennis, golf and other money intensive recreations.

In South Africa the Black man took to soccer like a fish to water. Mining companies, city councils and the Government saw to it that there were enough ponds for these soccer dolphins. In Soweto, near Johannesburg, the biggest Black city south of Lagos, they come in their thousands on Sundays to watch league matches. Sometimes tempers run hot and fights flare up on the spectator stands. There is a certain South American fanaticism among South Africa's Blacks when it comes to 'fussi ball'.

In 1955 the non-White South Africa Soccer Federation (SASF) made representations to the Federation of International Football Associations (FIFA). Run by Coloureds and Indians and claiming some Black membership, the SASF argued that it should be recognized internationally instead of its White South African counterpart, the Football Association of South Africa (FASA). SASF shunned offers of affiliation with the White FASA and five years later it managed to move FIFA to issue an ultimatum to the White soccer administrators in South Africa : integrate or be damned. At that stage FASA was already affiliated with the largest local Black soccer organization, the SA Bantu Football Association.

Yet in 1961 FIFA suspended FASA, which meant that South Africa could no longer take part in international soccer fixtures. In the ensuing years the politically motivated SASF, having lost almost all its initial Black support, campaigned strongly for complete ostracism of South Africa by the world football administrators. Eventually, at FIFA's Frankfurt Congress in June 1974 it took exactly ten minutes to have South Africa pushed within boot-lace distance from final expulsion. The newly appointed Secretary-General of Africa's Supreme Council for Sport, Jean-Claude Ganga of Brazzaville, was on the scene to express his supreme satisfaction and to predict South Africa's final ouster 'latest, by the 1976 Congress in Montreal'. The politically motivated non-White minority in South Africa at long last accomplished its political goals with the assistance of Black Africa, the Arabs and a few minor league Communists. They had reason to celebrate, while Black South African soccer chief George Thabe, representing 400,000 players, murmured : 'We're out. No reason, very little logic and a lot of politics. FIFA has become worse than the United Nations and even totally multi-racial football will not help South Africa.' Representing the vast majority of South Africa's Black players who were already enjoying mixed competition at home, Thabe was anxious *not* to have his country and his own players excluded from world competition, but was not given the opportunity to argue his case at the world meeting.

As if to be sure that Thabe did not leave Frankfurt with any misgivings about the no-foul rules applying to soccer politics in the seventies, he was treated to the sight of FIFA President Sir Stanley Rous being booted out in a not-too-gentle fashion by

Brazilian multi-millionaire Joao Havelange. *To the Point* reported from Frankfurt : 'Surprisingly, Havelange led in a second ballot (56 nations, mainly European, wanted Rous again) but his three-year R 1 million wooing of 84 national associations, many of them African and Asian, paid off. The Brazilian, who apparently paid the fares of many African delegates to secure their vote, had become FIFA's seventh President, the first outside Europe.'

'European dismay at Havelange's bought election, cheered by Latin-American delegates and journalists, evoked a gruff "Now, let's see him make good on those African and Asian promises" from a "disgusted" German official', according to *To the Point*. Rous himself, when handed a bouquet to mark the award of an honourary life presidency, said : 'I feel as if I've been handed a wreath.' Two wreaths. One for Rous and one for South Africa. Cut from the same flower bed. Rous, the sometime champion for the retention of South Africa, was out of the way. In his place stood Havelange—heavily obligated to Black Africa for its voting support.

In 1955 when it all started, the average White South African sports enthusiast could not be bothered about being deprived of international competition in soccer. Rugby and cricket are national sports—not soccer. But the principle—or the lack of it— had them worried. If South Africa could be booted out of FIFA for purely political reasons, the same could happen in other sports. Also, as the drawn-out battle for South Africa's continued membership of FIFA developed, soccer rapidly gained a larger following until mixed tournaments in the early seventies could count on 50,000 spectators at a time. And then there was Dennis Brutus, a Coloured teacher with a flair for agitation and a fine palate for the doctrines of the left.

In October 1962 the South African Non-Racial Olympic Committee (SANROC) was launched by Brutus in opposition to the officially recognized South African Olympic and National Games Association (SAONGA). SANROC's aim was ostensibly to bring about full integration in South African sports—right down to club level. In reality its drive proved to be one for a change of government at the tip of the African continent. Brutus intends for South Africa a people's revolution and a Communist-backed socialist state. Sport simply served as a splendid guise. Proscribed under the Suppression of Communism Act for illegal activity in Johannesburg, Brutus got John Harris to deputize for him in SANROC. Sandwiched between overseas meetings and all-round fielding for SANROC, Harris managed to do his bit for the so-called African Resistance Movement as well. It was in the name of the latter group that he planted a bomb at Johannesburg station that killed and maimed several unsuspecting victims.

After serving his sentence Brutus emigrated to London. Recruiting a few dedicated lieutenants, he established SANROC-in-Exile and set about travelling the world to spread his message. The Supreme Council for Sport in Africa and the Communist world embraced his cause wholeheartedly. Innsbruck, Tokyo, Rome, Copenhagen, Teheran, Grenoble, Lausanne, Warsaw, Dubrovnik and finally Amsterdam were milestones on the road.

In 1963, under severe pressure from SANROC and its Afro-Asian and Communist allies, the International Olympic Committee sent South Africa an ultimatum : Integrate or run the risk of being barred from the Tokyo Games. The South African officials countered by submitting to the IOC the names of at least seven non-Whites who would be included in their team for Tokyo. The IOC—still programmed by the Afro-Asians and SANROC—came up with a new demand that the South African sports administrators should publicly dissociate themselves from their Government's policy of apartheid before they could qualify for the Olympics.

This was one demand that SAONGA could not meet. They, as apolitical sport administrators, were simply not ready to denounce their own Government on political grounds. As they saw the gates on Tokyo Olympic village being shut in their faces— and that of several outstanding South African non-White athletes—Frank Braun and the other executives of the South African Olympic and National Games Association (also sometimes referred to as SANOC) could not help but notice the irony of it all. On the inside were many African one-party states where any sign of opposition even from legitimate *bona fide* politicians was suppressed. And imagine the Russian sport industry reprimanding its Government in public ! Yet these were the ones who shouted the loudest for South Africa's expulsion.

In 1966 at Rome the three SAONGA delegates once again assured the IOC that it accepted the Olympic Charter unconditionally. But it has already become abundantly clear that Brutus and his men and the Third World were not really interested in sport as an end in itself. They intended for South Africa radical political changes, because the existence of a Western Government in Africa's most viable territory was totally unacceptable to them and their Communist friends.

Still, SAONGA obtained the IOC's blessing for the formation of a joint liaison committee consisting of an equal number of Black and White representatives to select teams and handle other matters relating to the Olympic Games. In September 1967 an IOC fact-finding commission under the chairmanship of Lord Killanin (now President of the world organization) toured South Africa to investigate sporting facilities available to Blacks. Accompanying him were Sir Adetekumbo Ademola, Chief Justice of Nigeria, and Mr Reggie Alexander, President of Kenya's Olympic Association.

Although critical of the facilities available to Blacks in some centres, the Commission could not help but note the steps taken by the South African sports authorities to ensure that fully representative Olympic teams were selected. Also, they pointed out, most Black sportsmen and administrators did *not* want South Africa to be barred from the Olympics as they themselves wished to have the opportunity to participate. SANROC, Brutus and the African lobby at the IOC were an embarrassment to the very people they purported to represent.

In February 1968 the IOC convened at Grenoble. Three representatives of SAONGA turned up—four came to represent SANROC. In fact, Brutus and his men had been quite active during the months leading up to Grenoble, writing, for instance, letters to each of some eighty Olympic Committees to dissuade them from lifting the ban on South Africa. SAONGA undertook to have mixed trials, select an integrated team on merit and to have them travel, march and compete under one flag. The IOC voted 38 to 27 for South Africa's re-admission to the Olympics—the votes against comprising the African, Asian and Communist blocs.

As has happened in the United Nations so often the African states simply refused to accept a vote as valid when it went against their expressed wish. They applied a tactic at which they proved to be past masters. One that rarely failed to bring about the desired changes : blackmail. At Brazzaville the Supreme Council for Sport in Africa convened to 'discuss' the matter. Thereafter one African country after another announced that it would boycott the next Olympic Games—to be held in Mexico City—if South Africa participated. Back in Johannesburg SAONGA was waiting in vain for an official invitation from the organizers of the Mexico City Olympiad.

The African threat gained support from Iraq, Syria, Saudi Arabia, India, Kuwait, the Soviet Union and even Italy. By mid-April nearly fifty countries had officially and unofficially expressed their opposition to South Africa's readmission. In America, Black athletes joined the boycott move. IOC President, Avery Brundage, tried to rationalise the whole sordid affair : 'We thought the safety of the South African team and the success of the Games were in grave doubt.' One of his Vice-Presidents, the Marquis of Exeter, was even more evasive. Some outside factors had come into the situation which made it 'most injudicious' for South Africans to go to Mexico, he explained.

The invitation from Mexico City never arrived. Instead the IOC launched a new vote on the whole issue, deciding to withdraw South Africa's invitation to the Games by 46 to 14 with 2 abstentions. The old UN formula had worked again. Black Africa wielded the big stick and all the world cowered into a corner. Proof perhaps that there is nothing noble, courageous or even moral in the world's attitude when it comes to a vote count. Black Africa could dominate the IOC as easily as the UN.

There was deep disappointment in South Africa, especially among Black athletes, such as middle-distance runner Humphrey Khosi, who were looking forward to their first Olympic Games. Barred from Mexico City because, it was said, their presence would lead to violence at the 1968 Games, these Black athletes and their White fellow team members must have found the opening days at the Mexican Olympiad rather ironic. For almost a week the police in Mexico City struggled to keep the lid on violent student demonstrations and finally Black Power adherents in the American team succeeded in introducing a sour racist note into the actual Games.

Then came the 1969 IOC meeting at Warsaw with Brutus and Company trying unsuccessfully to expel South Africa from the international organization altogether; and finally Amsterdam, where the ouster succeeded. Nobody knew for certain what clinched the issue at about 5 pm on that fateful Friday, 15 May 1970. When the IOC members adjourned for lunch soon after 1 pm, there was a clear impression that South Africa's prospects of staying in were quite favourable. After all, the facts were on her side. It could not simply have been Brutus's and his three assistants' lunch-hour work that accounted for the sudden switch. Floating votes obviously once again drifted to the opposition as a result of strong African pressure. And blackmail, no doubt, clinched the deal.

An IOC official, Constantin Adrianov, once pointed out that it is not countries and their governments which belong to the IOC, but National Olympic Committees. Yet South Africa's sports administrators and sportsmen were expelled because of a vendetta against their Government. Avery Brundage stated: 'The world has never been so peaceful as to be void of conflicts between countries and political systems. But if these conflicts were to penetrate the idea of the Olympic Games, their early end can be taken for granted.' They have penetrated 'the idea of the Olympic Games' in the case of South Africa and Rhodesia and nobody seems to have heeded Brundage's sage advice.

The same IOC that extracted all kinds of assurances from the South African Olympic and National Games Association that it would not discriminate in sport, ignored its own Rule 1, which states that there shall be no discrimination at the Olympic Games against any country or person on grounds of race, religion or political affiliation. Said South Africa's Prime Minister Vorster: 'I think it is presumption of the worst kind to dictate to us and say: "Before you do this, that and the other in South Africa, we shall not play with you. We shall pick up our marbles and go." This is the purest nonsense. I do not believe that giving way to people who take such presumptuous decisions is going to serve sport in any respect whatsoever.'

World-famous South African golfer, Gary Player concurred. If he had to choose between sport and the political future of his country, he said, he would have no hesitation in foregoing sport. Player hardly had to prove his *bona fides* as campaigner for equal opportunity in sport. While others were merely talking, he was actively engaged in helping Black golfers in South Africa and abroad. He had a lion's share in integrating tournaments in South Africa. In the annual South African PGA there are, for example, more Black participants to be seen than in any comparable US tournament. At the same time Player invited American Black golfer Lee Elder to play in South Africa, while assisting South African Black golfer Vincent Tshabalala to participate overseas. In the United States he is one of the persistent voices in favour of inviting a deserving Black golfer to the famous Augusta Masters tournament. Until 1974 the Masters remained an all-White affair.

The South African Olympic and National Games Association had to resign itself to the fact that the Olympic Games were out of bounds to their athletes for as long as Black Africa and her allies ruled the IOC. If our sportsmen can't go to the Games, they reasoned, we could still bring world-class athletes to South Africa and stage our own mini-Olympics. First in Cape Town at the end of 1971 and later in Pretoria during April 1973, SAONGA managed to stage fully-fledged integrated international events. Despite heavy pressure on world-class athletes to boycott these events—in some instances overseas competitors were actually threatened by their home authorities with expulsion and banning orders—hundreds attended.

The South African sports authorities showed their complete lack of prejudice by inviting, for example, athletes from such Black countries as Kenya where critical governments are situated. The Kenyan Government saw to it that Olympic medallists such as Kip Keino, Julius Sank and Ben Jipchoto were prevented from travelling to Pretoria. In the end nearly 900 athletes— Black, White and Asian—from five continents converged on the South African administrative capital to join the multi-racial throng. Brutus and his followers abroad noted these developments with disapproval.

An anti-Government Sunday newspaper in Johannesburg commented two days after South Africa's expulsion from the IOC: 'These fanatics foolishly believe that by getting South Africa expelled from international sport, by turning a cricket tour into a matter of crisis and conscience in Britain, by mobilizing Afro-Asian pressure against the Springboks, by making blackmail a new and dangerous weapon, they are serving the cause of non-Whites in this country. They are not.'

Dennis Brutus master-minded South Africa's expulsion from the International Olympic Committee. Assisted by his brother Wilfred, Chris de Broglio and a few other embittered 'exiles' he extended his efforts to other areas, like cricket and rugby. And in Peter Hain he found a useful ally in 1970. Hain and Brutus were no strangers. Back in the good old days in South Africa they shared mutual friends.

The same John Harris who deputized for Brutus in SANROC when he had trouble with the authorities was also an intimate friend of the Hain family. Harris was a member of the Liberal Party and Walter Hain the Chairman of the Pretoria branch of the Party. Harris was tried, convicted and sentenced to death for leaving a bomb in the Johannesburg railway station which killed a woman and injured many passengers.

A petition for clemency sponsored by Harris's wife and the Hains was signed by only about 300 people and failed. Harris was hanged at 5.30 am on 1 April 1965. His body was taken to the Pretoria West cemetery where it was cremated. Enter Peter Hain, dressed in a school blazer and grey flannel trousers. He spoke with a quivering voice. Harris, the station bomb-killer, was his hero. 'We are here to say farewell to John Harris, whom we all loved,' he said. He quoted from John Donne and from Matthew, Chapter 5 . . . 'Blessed are they who are persecuted for righteousness' sake, for theirs is the Kingdom of Heaven.' (This quotation led to bitter attacks in the South African press. Surely, it was contended, it was the victims of the bomb outrage who suffered persecution.) Hain also read from Ecclesiastes, Chapter 3 . . . 'A time to kill and a time to heal: a time to break down and a time to build up.' Then he led the small gathering in singing 'We'll walk hand in hand hand some day'.

Not surprisingly, the backlash of the bomb outrage and support for Harris by the Hains severely damaged Alan Paton's Liberal Party. Mrs Harris and her eighteen-month-old son left South Africa for England by boat in March 1966. Her travelling companions were Mr and Mrs Hain and their four children, Peter, Tom, Joanne and Sally. Peter Hain had all the makings of an active agent for anti-South African causes and nobody was surprised when he and some friends surfaced at Basildon during July 1969 to disrupt a cricket match between an English side and a visiting South African team.

That same month Hain was one of those who ran on to the tennis courts at Bristol to stop play between South Africa and England in a Davis Cup match. 'I was held in prison for a few hours . . . we just didn't know our rights then,' Hain reminisced later. An intelligent student and shrewd operator, Hain quickly found out that for demonstrators there was no problem in trampling on others' rights without having their own freedom curtailed.

He picked up a few worthwhile tips from veteran sports-buster Dennis Brutus. With two South Africa exclusions at Tokyo and Mexico City, as well as the 1968 British cricket tour cancellation, to his credit, Brutus stood unchallenged as the champion. Jet-setting from continent to continent to organize international sport boycotts against South Africa, he managed to steal a few moments in between to train Hain. On 10 September 1969, in the thick of the Stop the Seventy Tour campaign, aimed against the proposed visit to Britain by a South African cricket team, a London *Telegraph* newsman told Hain : 'You're blackmailing everyone.' Hain's education was complete.

The 1969 visit to Britain by the Springbok rugby team served as a dress rehearsal for the 1970 South African cricket tour of Britain . . . which Hain and his following aimed to stop. Assisting Hain with his assault on the South African rugby giants were men like Father Trevor Huddleston,[2] Father Ambrose Reeves, Liberal MP David Steel, leftist student leader Jack Straw and Louis Eaks. The latter—Hain's twenty-four-year-old confidant —did not stay around for too long. On record as having toured Algeria, where he allegedly conspired with Palestinian terrorists, it was not Eak's political career that led to his downfall. In August 1970 he was tried and convicted for having committed an indecent act with another man.

The Springbok rugby players could never escape the sports-busters. They were constantly harassing the visiting sportsmen— in their hotels, in buses and on the rugby fields. Taunting, abusive and provocative. Spoiling for a fight—an incident that would show up these athletes as intolerant racists. Twickenham, where the 'Boks played the London Counties, provided the typical example. Outside the stadium there were some 2,000 demon-strators carrying the usual placards and shouting the usual slogans—'Get Out !' . . . 'Go home !' . . . 'Sack Vorster' . . . 'Kill

2. Huddleston, author of *Naught for Your Comfort*, gained prominence in South Africa in the late fifties as a bitter opponent of the Government's Black slum-clearance programme.

the Boers!' . . . 'Stop the match'. Four-letter jargon abounded. Inside another contingent moved into a strategic corner.

A reporter of South Africa's *Scope* magazine was on the scene. He wrote: 'Then the cheer went up and the Springboks in their green and gold ran on to the field—fit and clean-cut and in striking contrast to the bearded, long-haired rowdies. . . . No other team in the history of sport had been victimized to the extent that they had, non-political men all, brought here solely by their love for and expertise in South Africa's national sport, they had nevertheless been made the target for all Britain's anti-South African wrath. Scapegoats for as ill-conceived an assortment of fanatic odd-balls as you can hope to gather in a country that smiles tolerantly on the "democratic right of the individual to demonstrate his preference"—yet a country which was already showing the first signs of concern for the obvious clash between the minority's right to demonstrate and the majority's right to watch a game of their choice in peace.'

The despatch continued: 'The usual formalities having been dispensed with, the two sides squared up for the match. At this moment there was a commotion on one side of the field. Some of the demonstrators had broken through the police cordon and were running on to the field, trailing behind them a handful of flustered bobbies.' One of these long-haired youths took up position right in front of South African Tonie Roux, standing some distance from the other players.

'From the spectators' stand it was impossible to hear what was said, but it was obvious that the young demonstrator, looking like a pint-sized puppet from a Greenwich Village freak-out in front of the Springbok, was a very excited demonstrator indeed. . . . One needs no imagination to know what he was saying to Roux, shaking his bony fist under the Springbok's nose and shouting at the top of his voice until he was hauled off by two policemen to the thunderous applause of the crowd.

'Those South Africans that were there will never forget the sight of Tonie Roux and the hippie. There was the little man, pregnant with pent-up venom against a country he had probably never seen, shouting abuse at a man that looked twice his size—and all the time Roux stood there, warming up, for all the world like a man alone, seemingly totally unaware of the nuisance in front of him. . . . Had he dealt that single blow every spectator was praying for, that blow would have gone down in the books as the blow that stopped the tour. . . . It would have given the demonstrators exactly what they wanted.'

In Swansea the Hain hordes succeeded in provoking a fight with policemen and spectators. Thirty of them and ten policemen —one with a stab wound in his breast—ended up in hospital. Charges of police brutality were bandied about by the disrupters. In all, according to Peter Hain's own body count, some 30,000 participated in his 'Bash a Boer' campaign during the rugby tour. Whitehall was showing signs of fear. Harold Wilson's Labour Government was beginning to express reservations about the advisability of a 1970 South African cricket tour. The dress rehearsal was a sound success.

Like Brutus, Hain found a willing ally in the Supreme Council for Sport in Africa. The Council went on record as saying that it would not hesitate to boycott the Commonwealth Games in Edinburgh should Britain dare to receive the South African cricketers. This blackmail and Hain's threat of violence and disruption brought swift results. Prime Minister Harold Wilson hastened to appear on television, urging the MCC to withdraw the invitation to South Africa. In so doing, he pleaded, they would save the Commonwealth Games and Britain. His Home Secretary, James Callaghan, ordered the Chairman and Secretary of the MCC to his office and in a three-hour meeting urged them to call off the whole affair in the public interest.

Eight days before the South Africans were due to arrive, the tour was cancelled by the MCC. Explained the Secretary, Billy Griffith, at a press conference in the Long Room at Lords : 'We discussed the matter fully and came to the conclusion that there was no alternative.' An MCC member said : 'It would have meant rebuffing the Queen as figurehead of the Government if we had not cancelled the tour.'

The MCC, said Mr Wilson, should not feel that they were being blackmailed or pressured by anyone, either because of the threat of demonstrations or because of the Commonwealth Games. 'After all, we always respect a sporting declaration. We respect the man who starts to walk to the pavilion without waiting for the umpire's finger.' Some newspapers were not fooled by such talk. Said the *Sunday Telegraph* : 'Mr Hain has besmirched our national game, given a political tinge to delicate race relations, salved the consciences of liberal bishops and . . . set a precedent for mob law under our present rulers. It is a formidable achievement, but one that is cruelly irrelevant to the cause he claims to have at heart.'

The *Daily Express* in London commented under the heading, THIS IS HOW BLACKMAIL WORKS : 'Once you have paid him the danegeld, you never get rid of the Dane.' These words of Kipling's, illustrating the folly of trying to buy off aggressors, echo with special significance today. The bully-boys who succeeded in having the Springbok cricket tour banned now plan to disrupt banks and firms doing business with South Africa . . . surrender by the authorities to their threats has fed their appetites. Britain will indeed rue the day this Government started to pay danegeld.'

In a crowded upstairs room at a Fleet Street public house Hain called a news conference : 'This is not the end,' he said. 'The movement will go on.' Sitting with him in the glare of television lights was Dennis Brutus, Chairman of SANROC. Like his tutor Brutus, Hain was now ready to go international. His first target was the 1971 Springbok rugby tour of Australia. The same formula, he argued, that worked in Britain, would also bring results in Australia. First there were serious disruptions and demonstrations with Australian policemen out in force to keep order. The trade unions joined in with boycott threats against airlines, hotels and restaurants daring to house, transport or feed the South Africans. Peter Hain was there to guide and assist.

Once again the assault on South Africa's rugby team had the desired effect. A few months later the proposed tour of Australia by the South African cricket team was cancelled. The *Sydney Morning Herald* described this cancellation as a triumph of force and authoritarianism. 'Great numbers of Australians must feel deep disquiet that the Board of Control has been compelled to retreat because of the threats of violence and disruption coming from a small but ruthless minority', it said. 'The authoritarian minority naturally will be elated. They will see the Board's decision as a vindication of their ugly tactics against the South African footballers.'

Hain's attention shifted to New Zealand. Like Australia with its CARIS (Campaign Against Racialism in Sport), New Zealand's spoilers also had an acronymic name to rally around —HART (Halt All Racist Tours). In 1970 Brutus made a 'lightning visit' to New Zealand at the invitation of Trevor Richards, Chairman of HART, to beef up their protest against the proposed New Zealand rugby tour of South Africa. They failed to stop the All Blacks—including several Maori players—from going to South Africa. In 1972 Richards flew to London to consult Hain about the best tactics to stop the 1973 Springbok rugby tour of New Zealand.

Although New Zealand Prime Minister Marshall had given notice that he would not yield to threats and demands by a handful of loud-mouthed demonstrators, and the Leader of the Opposition Labour Party, Norman Kirk, promised not to interfere, the situation quickly changed. A few months before the general election in 1972 Kirk explained : 'The Labour Party is not in the business of directing private organizations who are acting within the law. We do not believe that limiting the freedom of New Zealanders will extend the freedom of others. Surely that is the difference between a democratic and a totalitarian society. In a totalitarian society, writing, art, culture and even sport is government-directed and politically oriented. In a democratic society there is an inalienable right to freedom of speech, art, writing, cultural and sporting pursuits.'

Early in 1973 Kirk, then Prime Minister after a victory at the polls, directed the New Zealand Rugby Football Union to withdraw its invitation to the Springbok Rugby Team. Some argued that the New Zealand Prime Minister had no choice. After all, HART and CARE (Citizens Association for Racial Equality) were training as early as December 1972 for disorder, disruption and violence at rugby matches. A disorderly group of anarchists, Trotskyists and other hyper-radical elements were being credited with starting rumours about possible dynamite attacks. And then there was the 1974 Christchurch Commonwealth Games with Black Africa's Supreme Council for Sport once again threatening a boycott should New Zealand dare to receive the South Africans.

Others maintained that Kirk would have acted regardless of these pressures, because his hue was that of a Harold Wilson—tainted strongly against anything South African. Kirk surprised even the radical demonstrators with his fervour in closing up all the cracks to prevent a single South African athlete from slipping through to his territory. He barred a South African women's tennis team from participating in the World Federation Cup tournament in New Zealand, sacrificing the tournament itself. The International Lawn Tennis Federation simply switched to another venue to allow the former world champion, South Africa, to participate.

Next, Prime Minister Kirk involved himself in drawn-out correspondence with the New Zealand Women's Bowling Association to prevent a South African team from entering for the world championships. He maintained that the White South African team was racist. It was pointed out to him that Blacks in South Africa—and numerous other countries in Africa—did not play bowls as they were simply not interested in the game. In fact, Zambia, Kenya and other Black countries could only field all-White teams! And New Zealand herself had no Maoris and Australia no Aborigines in their line-up. Norman Kirk refused to listen. South Africa had to stay out.

By barring South Africa's rugby team from competing in New Zealand, Norman Kirk saved the Commonwealth Games. But, asked some, what about Uganda? Did not, after all, General Idi Amin promise all and sundry that only Black Africans would be considered fit for inclusion in his team? True, most of Idi's Asians were already hounded from Uganda and the few remaining souls were probably in no position to play games. But still, where was the principle of non-racism which Mr Kirk so religiously pursued? The New Zealand Prime Minister gave the assurance that he would not accept a racially selected Ugandan team. Such a team arrived, participated and left.

Opposition member Downie of Pakuranga raised the matter in the Wellington Parliament. How, he asked, did Mr Kirk reconcile his opposition to the Springbok tour with his 'Nelsonian-eye attitude' to the selection on racial grounds of a Maori rugby team to tour Fiji? 'The all-Maori team does not purport to be a national representative team,' retorted the Prime Minister. 'The all-White Springbok team does purport to be a representative South African side.' The slip was beginning to show. Never at any stage were there any claims that the Springbok rugby side represented more than simply White South Africa. Like the British home unions—England, Ireland, Wales and Scotland playing abroad on their own and not as a British side, the Springboks in their traditional rugby ties overseas represented only the

White people of South Africa. While a Maori side is not regarded as racist, why should a White side automatically be condemned as such?

The questioning in Parliament continued : what would the Prime Minister's reaction be to a rugby tour of New Zealand by the Proteas, a South African Coloured team? Answer : representing a group within South Africa it would be in the same category as the Maoris—and welcome.

The Kirk principle at last became crystal clear : a team was only racially selected when it happened to be White. If Black or Coloured or Maori it was acceptable as non-racist because racism happened to be a White phenomenon only—more particularly a White South African one. Undeterred, Mr Kirk moved on to squash rackets, surf life-saving and softball, nit-picking through every South African team list, raising objections, imposing bans. Hain himself could not have done it more assiduously.

Prime Minister MacMahon, who had the guts to stand up against the Springbok rugby tour-busters in 1971, lost out in the Australian election to socialist Gough Whitlam. Equally selective in the distribution of his indignation concerning racism, Whitlam refused transit facilities for all South African sports teams 'not selected on merit'. In his case also the question came up : What about Uganda? Somehow, in the typical fashion of some politicians evading important questions, he succeeded in having the all Black team (selected at trials open only to Black Ugandans) slip by on their way to the Commonwealth Games in New Zealand.

Like Kirk, Whitlam had no time for discrimination of any kind between races, especially when it concerned sport. It was therefore with some surprise that the world heard from Aboriginal Affairs Minister Cavanagh in June 1974 that his Government had set aside some 80,000 Australian dollars 'to help Aboriginal sports clubs and individual sportsmen'. Following the success of the Aboriginal football team's visit to Papua, New Guinea, said Cavanagh, it was decided to send an all-Aborigine cricket team on a similar tour. In official Australian eyes any distinction on sports fields in South Africa between Black and White remained evil, while these officials themselves were financially sponsoring and encouraging Aboriginal sports exclusiveness on their own soil. In 1974 Peter Hain and company were frantically at work trying to prevent the British Lions rugby team from touring South Africa. As in the past, Hain could count on the solid support of the Supreme Council for Sport in Africa. After a brief Conservative interlude Harold Wilson's Labour Government was back at 10 Downing Street and there was no reason, so they thought, why a threatened boycott by the African body should not bring the same swift success as in 1970, when Britain's cricket authorities had to cancel their series with South Africa. In that year the Supreme Council for Sport in Africa brought Labour Prime Minister Wilson and the British cricket administrators to heel by threatening to stay away from the coming Commonwealth Games in Edinburgh.

This time the British rugby authorities refused to pay the African extortionists, despite heavy pressures again from the Wilson Government and sections of the press. Most in Fleet Street were in favour of handing over the ransom—conjuring up morbid visions of future African sport and political reprisals if the rugby administrators refused. The rugger men stood firm. Said Albert Agar, Secretary of the Lions' tour committee, 'We won't give in to threats. There are so many people threatening things in the world today and it is time someone stood up to these threats.'

Doug Ibbotson of the *Evening News* was one of the few in Fleet Street who openly supported Agar's stand. Having made short work of Mr Hain, the writer turned his attention to Mr Jean Claude Ganga, Secretary-General of the Supreme Council for Sport in Africa, who sent the blackmail note to 10 Downing Street. Mr Ganga had said: 'If Britain send their team, it will be an act of support for South Africa . . .' To which Mr Ibbotson replied: 'My dear, deluded sir, Britain is not sending their team. The Lions are a party of sportsmen who support nothing but each other on the field of play and nothing else but their given right to play whom they choose, where they choose, and with open minds.'

Opposed to the tour, the *Guardian* could only mention one instance where the boycott would affect British-African sport relations: the scheduled appearance at Crystal Palace of the world 1,500-metre record holder, Filbert Bayi of Tanzania. Said Ibbotson: 'The mind boggles.' There was, it transpired, another event which was killed in retribution by Black Africa:

the proposed visit of thirty-five British soccer players who were invited to play a few exhibition matches in Zambia.

Shortly after the British Lions rugby team left for South Africa, the Wilson Government instructed its Ambassador in Pretoria not to have any social contact with these obstinate sportsmen. Declaring her own fellow countrymen lepers on foreign soil was about the best last-minute effort Joan Lestor, Junior Foreign Minister, could muster to appease Black Africa and Hain. Herself a former office-bearer of the Anti-Apartheid Movement, Miss Lestor followed up with apologies in person to the rulers of Zambia and Kenya.

Announced by the *Daily Mail* under the headline DON'T FEED THE LIONS, Miss Lestor's action was described by the former Conservative Minister of Sport, Eldon Griffiths, as a spiteful little gesture. 'That the British Lions will tremble in their boots at the thought of being denied a handshake by the Ambassador is surely a trifle ludicrous,' he said. Labelled by the *Daily Telegraph* as 'plain silly' and the *Daily Express* as 'petty, pathetic and sinister', Lestor's twisting of the Lions' tail also came as a disappointment to the Left-wing *Guardian*. She should have done more, the *Guardian* argued, as this action would not be strong enough to placate Black Africa.

From South Africa came word that the Lions were not too disturbed about the prospect of not being invited over to the British Embassy for drinks. Rugby officials explained : 'Our main reason in going to South Africa is to play rugby and the great thing is to cut down on entertainment if you possibly can.' The British team played rugby very well, returning to London, as they did, with an unbeaten record after having played eleven 'provincials' and seven internationals—four against the Springboks, one against Rhodesia, one against the Black Leopard team and one against the Coloured Protea team.

Opposition Leader Edward Heath was at London's Heathrow Airport to welcome the returning victors, with Labour Sports Minister, Dennis Howell, also in attendance. Against the rugby tour from the outset, Howell vacillated for days, but for obvious reasons eventually decided to join the welcoming party. Willy John McBride's rugby team was the first in almost a century to return undefeated from South Afirca.

In an elated Britain these thirty gladiators suddenly became precious propaganda property. Also waiting at the Airport Hotel were Hain and a few followers. His sister stepped forward and threw a flour-bomb at Heath—indicative perhaps of the pain felt in those circles at witnessing the sparkling champagne hospitality accorded the British Lions.

To add insult to injury, Bernard Levin of *The Times* suggested to Hain that he oppose the forthcoming London visit of the Bolshoi Ballet because of the 'racialist tyranny in Soviet Russia'. Dismissing it as sheerly impractical to oppose tyranny from 'every other quarter', Hain even attempted to rationalize Soviet Russia as a society without racial persecution. After all, he could add, ballet is not sport. Then another pundit proposed that Mr Hain get cracking on banning Britain from playing football against the Russians. Hain's defences were wearing thin and his double-standard practice against South Africa was beginning to be noticed even by erstwhile supporters.

In the late sixties American Negro tennis player Arthur Ashe applied for a visa to come and play in the South African Open Tennis Championships. It was refused. Reasons were given—an unusual practice for the South African authorities. Ashe, it was pointed out, was one of the prime movers of a resolution at the United Nations calling for a blanket sports ban on South Africa. He promised his friends to go to South Africa to put a 'crack in the apartheid wall'. Adding : 'I would like to drop an H-bomb on Johannesburg.' Ashe obviously preferred playing politics to swinging rackets at the South African Open.

The whole anti-apartheid industry went into operation to afford this visa refusal maximum publicity. Ample proof once again, they stated, that South Africa was blatantly racist and would not allow a Black sportsman to enter from outside. Lost in the excitement were all kinds of assurances by the South African authorities that skin colour had nothing to do with Ashe's ban. Even if he were White and said these things he would still have been barred, it was explained. As for Black sportsmen not being allowed, how about Aborigine Evonne Goolagong from Australia, Black American golfer Lee Elder, several Negro boxers, a Black rugby player from France and dozens of other Coloured athletes who competed freely in South Africa?

But the anti-lobby was not in a mood for listening. It played the Ashe affair for months and then revived it almost on an annual basis. Foremost among the American lobbyists who castigated 'racist' South Africa for robbing poor Black Arthur of the opportunity to test his tennis skills against the world's best at Ellis Park, Johannesburg, were Black Congressman Charles Diggs and George Houser, Executive Director of the American Committee on Africa. Then came 1973. Ashe once again applied for a visa, promising this time to concentrate on sport and to refrain from political agitation. He was allowed in. On arrival at Jan Smuts Airport, Johannesburg, he was asked about his H-bomb statement : 'That was when I was a callow youth.'

The thirty-year-old Black American tennis player did not like everything he saw and nobody in South Africa took umbrage at his criticisms, which enjoyed wide publicity in the South African press. He lost in the finals against fellow American Jimmy Connors, hopped around the country on a quick familiarization tour and left for London—promising to return for the next tennis Open.

In August 1974 the *International Herald Tribune* reported that Ashe intended to play again in South Africa despite pressure by the President of the Supreme Council for Sport in Africa not to do so. 'Now I am going to tell him calmly, when I see him, that I disagree—little Arthur Ashe is going to go against the grain of all Black Africa and a lot of the militants here,' Ashe told the *Tribune*'s Washington correspondent. 'But boycotting South Africa is avoiding the fact, and it's not going to accomplish anything substantive.'

Two months later another tennis drama was unfolding on the centre court at Johannesburg's Ellis Park. South Africa defeated Italy in the semi-final for the Davis Cup, four to one, and was scheduled to meet the other finalist, India, within the next month. Word came from New Delhi that caste-ridden India would refuse to play South Africa until her Government promised to integrate on every level. Said Raj Khanna, Secretary of the All-India Lawn Tennis Federation, in declining South Africa's offer either to receive his team in Johannesburg or to play them in a neutral country—or any independent Black African country willing to stage the finals, 'we would in any event have won against South Africa, five to nil'.

Tennis buffs who knew the strength of the respective teams found this statement absurd. They contended that the opposite was much more likely. In previous individual non-Davis Cup matches against their opposite numbers from India, the South African players had always won. But such was the claim made by India when she opted out to leave South Africa with the Davis Cup in hand—winners by default. A vanquished victor.

In South Africa there are 60,000 registered White tennis players and 22,000 Blacks, Coloureds and Indians. The famous Sugar Circuit and other major tournaments are open to all races. Selection for the men's Davis Cup and women's Federation Cup teams is strictly on merit. Of the 22,000 non-White players, 20,000 are affiliated with the White union. They urged India to play South Africa. The other 2,000—3 per cent of South Africa's total tennis-playing population—insisted on a boycott. India preferred to listen to them.

As always irony and humour were elements in this saga of double-dealing. One sports commentator suggested—following on South Africa's proposal that an independent African country serve as the venue for the final—that Uganda be approached. (This is one country, but not the only one, in Africa which has deported her Indian citizens and banned all South Africans from entering.)

In South Africa at the same time as Ashe first strolled through Customs at Johannesburg's Jan Smuts Airport was Bob Foster. Defending his world light-heavyweight boxing title against a White South African contender, the American Negro enjoyed hospitality among both White and Black. At a fully integrated event he narrowly defeated Pierre Fourie. 'Before I came here I was cold towards South Africans,' said Foster afterwards. 'I thought in a different way. Now I love this place. It's great. I'll be glad to come back.'

Said another visitor, Pakistani cricketer Billy Ibadulla: 'I have read much about the country in newspapers and magazines, but I don't think you can get true impressions until you come here.' He said foreign Black visitors should be encouraged to come to South Africa. There were some abroad who disagreed vehemently. The true impression was exactly what bothered them.

Charles Diggs, the Detroit undertaker, for example, slammed the Ashe and Foster visits as 'the highest form of deception'. Such 'mixed sport gestures' by the South African Government would not change the political situation. Added George Houser of the ACA: 'It is a mistake for Arthur Ashe and Bob Foster to go. It helps South Africa to chalk up a public relations victory without changing the basic pattern and evil of apartheid.' In London a leading official of the Anti-Apartheid Movement who also dabbled in sport demos, Abdul Minty, summed up : 'Even when South Africa has integrated sport, we would not be satisfied. What we want is a Black government.'

So the cat was out of the bag. As Y. C. Meer, Indian President of the South African Soccer Federation, put it : 'At the moment sport is a ball being kicked around in a political game.' To those who followed Brutus, Hain and others closely this hardly came as a shocking revelation. After all, Dennis Brutus struck upon the sports boycott idea not because he was an avid athlete deprived of opportunities, but as a politician banned under the Suppression of Communism Act in South Africa. At that time South Africa's enemies at the United Nations and the World Court of Justice were experiencing serious set-backs in their offensive to topple the hated 'White regime'. Brutus suggested sport as a more likely arena for instant success. A South Africa isolated in sport, he contended, would be more easily won over because next to politics that was *the* most important facet of South African life.

In essence, then, there were no real differences between the efforts at the UN to crush White South Africa, the attempts at the World Council of Churches to obliterate the present rulers or the campaign at the IOC and other world sport bodies. The tactics were the same and the players often identical. When the World Court decided in favour of South Africa, the decision was ignored, then reversed by OAU and Communist bloc political manoeuvring and by packing the court itself. When South Africa was readmitted on merit to the Olympics, blackmail threats from the OAU managed to reverse the decision.

The prestigious *Chicago Tribune* summed up as follows shortly after South Africa was finally ousted from the 1968 Mexico City Games. 'South Africa's conciliatory attitude failed to appease the Communists and the Black African nations, which are always seeking to make political capital out of racial separation in South Africa . . . Now the policy of keeping politics out of sport has been discarded and the Communist bloc and the African mini-states and non-states have won the day—an unhappy day, to be sure; another day of mourning.'

The *Tribune* condemned the United States for not speaking up

146

against the black-balling of South Africa. 'For the United States this is another craven retreat. Again we have been unable to face up to the Communists, and again we have truckled to the prejudices of the anarchic countries of Black Africa.' The *New York Times* concurred: 'The fact that the Olympic board chose to ignore is that South Africa did retreat significantly from its normal segregation practices in the effort to gain readmission into the Games. . . . This was a major victory for the African countries and their Sovet bloc and other allies—a victory that will encourage the use of similar tactics in other international bodies including the United Nations.'

While ping-pong served to open cobwebbed doors between Red China and the United States, political arguments about sport are used to block the passageways between South Africa and the rest of the world. A South African flag ripped to shreds at an international surf life-saving contest in Australia; a bunch of unkempt demonstrators squatting on a Stockholm tennis court to stop play between the South African and Swedish Davis Cup teams; security guards screening Gary Player from public view as he strolls down the fairways of American golf courses; a South African squash team playing Test matches in Britain at secret venues to dodge demonstrators; and hooligans shouting abuse at a Coloured South African rugby team touring Britain. These are all manifestations of the effort to isolate and bleed South Africa to death.

Changes are taking place in South African sport. Some argue that many of these are indirectly, if not directly, a result of the pressure from Hain and others. A sure sign, they say, that all their efforts were not in vain. Others maintain that the politically motivated Hain hordes and Brutus brutes had little effect on Souh Africa—a country which sets its own pace according to the dictates of its own situation. Be that as it may, the winds of change are wafting through the sporting life of the country. In some sports, such as soccer and cycling, Black and White have equal representation on control boards. In others, like cricket, integrated play even at club level is anticipated.

Reports under headings such as THE SAD FACE OF SOUTH AFRICAN SPORT and STEADY MOVE TO SPORT ISOLATION still appear in the South African press, although somewhat less frequently than before. A list of the sports in which South Africa finds herself excluded from world competition fluctuates like the readings on the stock exchange. South Africa still manages every year to attract some forty teams in various sporting spheres from abroad and to arrange an equal number of visits for her own sportsmen overseas. The isolation is still far from complete and everyone expects the sport-busters to continue their agitation, threats, disruption and blackmail.

Brutus, Hain and Minty anticipated that major political changes would follow their sports campaign against South Africa. They obviously misread the situation. Speaking in Parliament, Prime Minister John Vorster, who plays to a thirteen golf handicap, spoke in his usual unequivocal fashion: 'Regarding our sports policy, my point of departure is that I am not adopting a policy to appease the world, but that I am adopting a policy for the people of South Africa and for the situation as it develops in South Africa. I am not insensitive to the attitude of the outside world. However, I am not prepared to lay down a policy which would satisfy the Anti-Apartheid Movement. I cannot and do not want to lay down a policy which would satisfy the Sports Council of Africa. I am not prepared to lay down a policy which would satisfy the Communists.'

Few in South Africa disagree with this statement. But does this mean that South Africa is intent on following a hard-line approach, barring mixed sport in any form? Scarcely.

Announcing an all-race knockout competition between the top soccer clubs, Sport Minister Piet Koornhof pointed out in October 1974 that in 76 of the 78 sports played in South Africa, mixed teams could be selected to represent the country. Cricket and rugby, where traditional ties existed between White South Africa and overseas opponents, were still exceptions.

He added: 'The policy of the South African Government is based on the acceptance and recognition of the various peoples living in South Africa and the whole basis of our policy as it applies to sport is to give all peoples the opportunity to compete in international sport, regardless of race and colour. Where discrimination on grounds of race and colour might still apply, the stated basis and object of our policy is to move away from it.'

Sports enthusiasts found this approach by Dr Koornhof reasonable. But not the Hains and the Brutuses and the Gangas. After all, they have never been particularly enthusiastic about sport.

# 7

# Nothing Can Now Be Believed

On 8 July 1974 *Time* magazine's cover story dealt with the press. Almost everybody (at least among journalists), said *Time*, remembers Jefferson's famous remark that, if he had to choose between a government without newspapers and newspapers without a government he would pick the latter. Added *Time*: 'But few recall that Jefferson also wrote on another occasion: "Nothing can now be believed which is seen in a newspaper." ' Public opinion polls were at that juncture, showing a steep erosion in the American reading public's belief in their own media.

In South Africa there is also a penchant for Jefferson's second—and less frequently used—remark, especially with regard to the world press. Subjected to an endless series of attacks, South Africans have come to regard the world press as a vicious monster bent on shouting and writing their country out of existence.

Black children scrambling for coins dropped in a garbage can by enterprising journalists become examples of deprivation. Black mineworkers secured to rocky slopes down a gold mine to prevent them from slipping were paraded in glossy magazines overseas as slave workers chained to their jobs. Sharp practice of this kind has created a positive mediaphobia in South Africa.

In the fifties South Africa appointed a distinguished body of men to determine exactly how bad foreign press coverage on her affairs was. Judges and politicians, these commissioners embarked upon a tedious word-count expedition. Stated the Commission of Inquiry after finger-tipping through 321,674 United Press cabled words dating from 1950 through 1955 : Of the news despatched 4.68 per cent was good, 21.58 per cent was faulty, 19.93 per cent was bad and 53.81 per cent was very bad.

Other agencies and newspapers received even worse ratings. The Commission found that over 90 per cent of the news despatched to the *New York Times* was very bad (3.01 per cent was good). Nearly 100 per cent of the items sent to *Time* Inc. was very bad. Figures for the British press were equally discouraging. So were data on Australia, New Zealand and Canada, with Germany, France and other non-English-speaking countries receiving a slightly more balanced view of South Africa through their own press.

The average South African sees the world press as downright dishonest—all of it. A monstrous lying machine. But those who have made a careful study of this phenomenon know that this popular view of the foreign press is in itself a case of gross over-simplification and distortion. Only a minor portion of the reporting done on South Africa is faulty. The press does not have to lie to damage a country's reputation—or an individual's. Truth can be quite honestly perverted by concentrating on the negative to the almost complete exclusion of the positive.

Some communications experts call this process one of selective negativity. Others describe it as advocacy journalism. The newsman sets out with a point to make and openly selects and some-times even tailors his material to fit. The same gentleman who ordinarily pays lip-service to 'objective reporting' loses all sense of fair play over South Africa in general and apartheid in particular.

Analysing world news coverage during the first five years of the fifties, South Africa's Press Commission discovered that the pro-Government voices seldom rated mention, while opposition voices were amplified almost beyond recognition. Insignificant dissenters were frequently transformed into important spokesmen, while small protest gatherings became milestone mass meetings, driving a beleaguered Government into a corner. While the South African Government was rapidly gaining strength at every new election, the overseas reader was assured and reassured at regular intervals that the end was near.

In the turbulent early sixties—the Sharpeville months—these

prophets of doom were stomping around South Africa in great excitement. At last, it seemed, the end *had* arrived. With sixty-seven Blacks killed instantaneously and many wounded by heavily outnumbered White police in a tragic skirmish at Sharpeville, near Johannesburg, these men of words sat poised for the final act; a partisan audience ready to applaud the end of the White South African and especially the hated Afrikaner. In their despatches there was nothing said on behalf of the White ruler and not an inch of space for him to speak up for himself.

In these difficult months, the Press Commission found, the utterances of the South African Government and statements by the police 'found virtually no place in the reporting' of large sections of the world press. Reports were often blindly in favour of the Black demonstrators, and the few side-references to Government views and policy were calculated not to inform but to ridicule and slander. A police denial, for example, backed by official enquiries, that dum-dum bullets were used to shoot the Black demonstrators at Sharpeville, was summarily dismissed by some reporters as a lie.

Norman Phillips was an obscure Foreign Editor on the *Toronto Daily Star* when Sharpeville shock-waved around the globe. On 21 March 1960, the day of the shooting, Phillips boarded a Johannesburg-bound aircraft to join the throng of newsmen converging on South Africa. Phillips left with explicit instructions, confirmed by cable from his Toronto headquarters soon after he unpacked in his Johannesburg hotel: 'Give us the blood and guts.'

He did not disappoint. So intent was he to satisfy his paper's every wish that he even ventured into a first-hand 'battle scene' account of a bloody riot in Cape Town while himself living in the relative ease of his medium-class Durban hotel room—almost 700 miles away. The only small problem was that some of these events never took place. Phillips was detained in jail under special emergency orders until the next flight left for Canada. In a matter of months after his hero's welcome in Toronto, his 'war diary' appeared under the title *The Tragedy of Apartheid*. Said one reviewer: 'Norman Phillips' book reminds one of Steinbeck's *Grapes of Wrath*.'

Overplaying his hand somewhat, Mr Phillips earned special mentions in his own country—and South Africa. His approach, however, was not very different from those of most of his fellow journalists at the time. The rule of the game was simple and straightforward : Praise the protesters and abuse the authorities. So obvious was this slant that even a relatively small Canadian daily felt a word of caution was necessary. Said the *Fredericton Gleaner* : 'Every Negro demonstrator against the laws of the Union [of South Africa] is inculpable and every policeman a headbreaker. That is the tenor of the stories we receive and publish from big news agencies. Take this despatch from Cape Town : "Troops and police clubbed hundreds of Negroes in the Cape Town area today when the Negroes failed to join a native back-to-work movement. Police also staged house-to-house raids and shooting was heard in one Negro township". Why are police doing this—if they were doing it', asked the *Gleaner*. 'The despatch does not say. It gives a grim story from the rioters' point of view and lets it go at that. Granted the South African situation is a bad one. The majority of Canadians are opposed to the policy of apartheid. But this gives more reason than ever for straight unbiased news reporting. And that, here in Canada, we are not getting. We trust our readers are searching between the lines as we are.'

The *New York Times* editorial department had no time for a between-the-lines expedition. On 6 April, 1960 it expressed indignation at continuing reports that Blacks in Cape Town were 'being forced back to work by police use of clubs, whips and guns'. These were in fact the methods used by the ringleaders of the rebels to prevent Blacks from crossing picket lines. On 21 April the *New York Times* discovered what the *Gleaner* suspected all along, namely, that reports of police beatings were highly exaggerated and inaccurate. 'The large mass of Africans', stated the *Times*, 'ignored the strike call and flocked back to work and school.' It was the strike leaders and not the police who had reason to intimidate and coerce.

This deliberate misrepresentation of South Africa by the overseas press is not a recent affair. In the immediate post-war years South Africa, under the leadership of the internationally popular General Smuts, found herself suddenly in the dock. For an honourable member nation of the world community and her Prime Minister this overnight switch from popularity was a traumatic experience. After all, Smuts was, more than any other single world statesman, responsible for the establishment of the United Nations. His ideals for mankind are embedded in the preamble to the UN Charter, which he himself wrote. South Africa, a relatively small member of the alliance, played a significant role in the war against the Axis powers—Ethiopia's liberation, for example, was accomplished largely by South African troops.

As early as 21 July 1946, the *Johannesburg Sunday Express* editorialized as follows, under the heading WHAT IS SOUTH AFRICA'S REPUTATION ABROAD?: '*The New Statesman* and other liberal journals in Britain habitually condemn the South African Government of Gen. Smuts and its people as "die-hard reactionaries". Indian propagandists are busy in London and New York picturing Natal as a new kind of ghetto. The gold industry is a favourite target of leftist writers overseas when they happen to think of South Africa.' Added the *Express*: 'The fact is that day in and day out South Africa is being presented in Britain and America as a country which persecutes its Indians, deliberately starves and tyrannizes its Natives and would like to grab the whole sub-continent to extend its nefarious policies.'

On 11 December 1947 Prime Minister Smuts was reported by the *Johannesburg Star* as saying that 'there is no country in the world with our prospects which has such poor publicity as we have'. Five months later Smuts and his United Party were beaten at the polls by Dr Daniel Malan and the Nationalists. Almost purely Afrikaans in make-up, the new Government presented the overseas media—especially the English ones—with a much easier target. During Smuts's so-called coalition rule it was rather difficult for the world press to blast away at the Afrikaners without also hitting English-speaking South Africa.

The tone of the new offensive was set by a London *Daily Express* reporter who flew to South Africa, shortly after the May 1948 election defeat for Smuts, to assess the damage on behalf of the British Empire. He cabled London: 'South Africa is in the grip of Nazi tyranny.' Despite the fact that 60 per cent of the South African troops who fought courageously and died valiantly on the side of the English-speaking world against the forces of Nazi Germany were Afrikaners, Malan and his supporters were pictured as arch-enemies of both Jew and Anglo-Saxon at home and abroad.

There was no way either in which the Afrikaner Nationalists could do right as far as the Black races in South Africa were concerned. The same South African English language press which complained during the years before 1948 that South Africa was unfairly criticized by those who did not understand her intricate racial problem now contended that it was Malan and his racial policy that was the cause of it all. In 1946 the *Sunday Express* reminded its readers that 'South Africa has grave racial and political problems which only she can solve, but her efforts to do so are being gravely embarrassed by a formidable and increasing mass of ill-informed and adverse opinion overseas'. Only four years later, with Malan in power, the *Johannesburg Star* contended that 'all the uproar and opprobrium have ensued since the Nationalists took office'. The former Smuts Government's policies, said the *Star*, 'did not involve South Africa in a clash with the rest of the world ... '.

The world press in the early years of Afrikaner Nationalist rule had a willing ally in South Africa's English-language press. Bent on regaining power for a government of its own liking, this local opposition press often provided deadly ammunition for the offensive from abroad. A *Natal Mercury* editorial on 18 September 1950 was typical of the message echoed abroad by the South African English press : 'What the Nationalists stand for is by now well known. Their one object is to transform a minority government into an Afrikaner republic, to subject the English-speaking section to an absolute and merciless dictatorship, to abolish the English language, to tear up the Constitution and by every underhand method to use South Africa for their purposes. If they can only manage to entrench themselves, the last vestige of freedom will disappear in this country. The Indian, the Native (Black) and Coloured will be dealt with and then they will deal with the English and those Afrikaners who do not subscribe to the Broederbond[1] creed. What will be the future of this country? Our state will be reduced to little less than slavery.'

None of these terrible forebodings came true, but the allegations stuck, distorting South Africa's picture abroad instead of toppling the Afrikaner Government. When eventually the South African English-language press realized that they were feeding

1. Allegedly an exclusive secret Afrikaner brotherhood bent on running the country.

the mouth that bites them from abroad it was too late. The myth had already become fact to a multitude in far-off lands. The nightmarish scarecrow image of South Africa which they helped to manufacture was frightening and infuriating peoples and nations to the ends of the earth. All South Africa's English-language press efforts to undo the story merely amounted to a feeble pulling at the jacket of this monstrous jackbooted figure.

A sampling of the world press in the years since May 1948, when Malan took over, shows vicious consistency in comment and coverage as far as South Africa was concerned. On 11 June 1948, for example, the New Zealand *Listener* heralded Malan's victory as follows: 'It may even be that democracy in South Africa is now holding a coat for fascism.' There were also forebodings of persecution of the Jews and 'harsher repression' of the 'Kaffirs and the Indians'.[1] On 8 October 1960 another New Zealand journal, the *Christchurch Press*, expressed fear for the future of their English-speaking brethren in 'Afrikaner dominated' South Africa: 'The Black victims of apartheid have their champions nearly everywhere; but perhaps more pitiful is the plight of the "English" South Africans who, through no fault other than regard for Britain, fear relegation to an outcast inarticulate minority.'

Commented one overseas pundit in Malan's time: 'There is the fear that the Nationalists plan a republic in which English-speaking South Africans will lose their language rights and be treated as second-class citizens.' Said another when Malan was succeeded by J. G. Strijdom as Prime Minister: 'He is openly anti-British. He is a fierce, demagogic and capable speaker, who is at his best or worst in his favourite language, Afrikaans—a rudimentary language not well adapted to the finer nuances of meaning.' Added a third: 'The two white races in South Africa are growing increasingly hostile to each other . . . there must be an end somehow to an unfruitful and sordid marriage which,

1. Malan's Government was actually one of the very first to recognise the new state of Israel. He was the first head of state to visit the newborn country. Commented the *Christchurch Press* on 10 July 1948: 'The New Zealand Prime Minister referred in Parliament to a horrifying example of want of unity in the Commonwealth:—No doubt the sudden South African recognition of the state of Israel'. Added the newspaper: 'The British Government is said to have been disconcerted.' Were these the actions of an anti-Semitic South Africa?

if continued, will surely end in disaster.' One journalist even claimed that the 'Union Jack pimple' was ripped out of the corner of the South African flag to satisfy Afrikaner demands.

At that very moment the same 'pitiful, inarticulate' English in South Africa were moving over to the National Government in large numbers as evidenced in landslide victories at the polls. Said the London *Times* on 4 February 1960 : 'The doctrine of unalterable inequality of races may be offensive to the British conscience, but the Afrikaner conscience applauds it.' And *Newsweek* wrote on 17 July 1961 : 'Down that fateful road that leads from freedom to tyranny marches the band of Afrikaner zealots who guide the destiny of South Africa.' But as Professor Dennis Worrall, a respected member of South Africa's English community pointed out, a lot of racial legislation blamed on the Afrikaner was framed, shaped and passed by the pre-1948 English-supported Government.

Declared the Australian *Melbourne Age* on Friday, 17 March 1961 : 'Racism has not been enforced so relentlessly since the days of Nazi Germany.' On that very day in neighbouring New Zealand the *Christchurch Press* described the Afrikaner 'government system' as 'far less akin to English democracy than to Hitlerian totalitarianism.' (No explanation was offered for the strange disturbance of police state peace in the form of regular Westminster-style elections in South Africa.)[3] There was obviously disagreement among leading members of the world press concerning the speed with which unhappy South Africa became authoritarian. While some concluded in 1948 that South Africa had become an instant dictatorship, others were still mentioning 'a drift towards a police state' in recent despatches on South Africa.

'Police state', 'Nazi', 'Fascism', 'Anti-Semitic'—these are still regulars in stories on South Africa. A supporting cast of Afrikaans words like *kragdadig*, *volk*, *kultuur* and *laager* serve to further strengthen the 'herrenvolk image' and to build resentment among readers and listeners abroad who do not understand their real meaning. Noted the South African Press Commission in the early sixties : The names of Afrikaner statesmen and leaders, where they have a Teutonic or Biblical origin and

3. At publication date South Africa was one of only eight countries in Africa that still allowed an opposition to function freely. The other thirty-five were under dictatorial rule.

an un-English sound, are generally used in conjunction with their surnames, even in those instances where these personalities are not usually referred to by these Christian names in public life in South Africa.[4] 'This is done, not only in order to create, through the use of the Teutonic sounding names, a resemblance between the National Party Afrikaner Government and the totalitarian regime of Germany under Hitler, but also to make these men appear strange, foreign and unacceptable to British readers.'

Every possible pretext is utilized to introduce the Nazi theme in writings on South Africa. In 1952 the *Guardian* found that 'the Commonwealth can have little common interest with a revival of Nazi beliefs' in South Africa. Ten years later the same newspaper was still at it. 'Unfortunately,' it said, 'the South African Government—like the Nazi Government—seems to fear the sane and civilized in its midst as if it has now given up the attempt to live by such standards.' In 1967 the London *Observer* took President Hastings Banda of Malawi to task for expressing the belief that South Africa was here to stay and that co-operation was imperative. 'That sounds dangerously like the European appeases who argued that Nazi Germany was invincible,' said the *Observer*. 'Apartheid—like Nazism—is bound, ultimately, to be destroyed.'

In 1967 Professor Edwin Munger, a world-renowned African expert from California, noted : 'As one who visited Nazi Germany before the war and got an inkling of the policy which led to the extermination of some six million Jews, it seems to me an insult to those who were gassed to suggest that South African official policy is worse. I am struck by the enthusiasm of South Africa for the Israeli cause—even stronger than in the United States. The seven million dollars contributed by Jews and many Afrikaners and the willingness of the South African Government to allow the transfer of such capital, in view of balance of payment problems, is a tribute to the warm-heartedness of South Africa for Israel.'

Since 1967—and especially during the Yom Kippur War of

4. The present South African Prime Minister is always referred to in his own country as John Vorster. Some elements in the South African English press and most of the foreign press seem stuck on his second Christian name, Balthazar.

1973—even more substantial financial support flowed from South Africa to Israel. Every year the South African Jewish Board of Deputies confirms in end-of-the-year reports that anti-Semitism is as insignificant in South Africa as anywhere else in the civilized Western world. Yet the Nazi image of South Africa persists. The world press would not let it die—even if it had to go to almost ridiculous neologistic lengths to keep it alive, as evidenced by Bernard Levin's description in the London *Times* of the activities of a South African Commission of Enquiry in March 1974 as '*Gestapoid* investigations'.

For British journalist Adam Raphael 1973 was a very good year. It all started in the United States where he attended Congressional hearings on the activities of American firms in South Africa. The issue was Black wages and apartheid. Reporting for the *Guardian* on the mounting pressure in America on businessmen to withdraw their investments from the land of apartheid, a thought occurred to the young obscure Mr Raphael : Why not investigate British business interests in South Africa as well?

He left for South Africa on a busman's holiday, visiting relatives in Cape Town and browsing around British industrial establishments. He was given *carte blanche* at many factory sites, yet afterwards he felt compelled to state that 'none of the firms were prepared to co-operate'. Explained Raphael : 'One book in particular which I used as a sort of basic text was *The South African Connection*.' This treatise was written by Communist Ruth First, Editor of the *Anti-Apartheid News*, Christabel Gurney, and Raphael's *Guardian* colleague, Jonathan Steele. Its basic premise : All investment in South Africa is evil.

Raphael's writings were, in essence, variations on the Ruth First theme. Black wages on the mines were described as 'near starvation level', despite mountains of free, calory-rich food heaped on these workers' plates three times a day. A new living quarter for Blacks in Windhoek he described as follows : 'It wouldn't do justice to a nineteenth-century prison.' Mr Raphael was not in the mood to be impressed with anything. Conclusion : In no other country in the world was the misery so great, and people so callously exploited, as in South Africa.

In a matter of weeks the *Guardian* published eight editorials under headings such as SCANDAL OF AFRICAN LABOUR, and TIME

TO AUDIT OUR SHAME AND SERFDOM IN SOUTH AFRICA. It became abundantly clear, as this campaign developed, that wages were not the major concern. It was simply a way of getting at South Africa and apartheid and of embarrassing British business into either fighting 'the system' or pulling out of the country. 'If British companies are unready to face their moral responsibilities—both in the wages they pay and their employment practices—the case for stopping all investment in South Africa will become overwhelming', contended the *Guardian*.

Other journals in Britain picked up the theme. In the second week of March 1973 thirty articles on Black wages in South Africa appeared in the Fleet Street press alone, and during the following week sixty-six. By the final week of March it soared to seventy-seven and during April one hundred and eighty-eight were published. 'The *Guardian* is to be congratulated for bringing into prominence the fact that well-known firms whose head offices or holding companies are in London are among the worst employers in South Africa', wrote the London *Times*. As in many other despatches on the wage controversy, Adam Raphael was also given personal credit in this instance.

The young unknown reporter from the *Guardian* had become the toast of Fleet Street and left-leaning London. Raphael stayed on top of the wave. He even managed to sneak in a second visit between an endless series of television and radio appearances and speaking engagements. On 3 July 1973 his efforts culminated in a two-and-a-half-foot-long editorial in the *Guardian*— perhaps the longest in its history—under the heading, SOUTH AFRICA : DOES BRITISH MONEY BOLSTER APARTHEID? In a free-swinging, wide-ranging attack on South Africa the *Guardian* concluded that 'the will of White South Africans to preserve apartheid may eventually be broken'.

The British Parliament took over where Mr Raphael signed off. The Rodgers Commission started probing Black wages in South Africa. British business found itself on the carpet, answering loaded questions on their treatment of Black labour. Proclaimed a headline in the *Guardian*, datelined Johannesburg and signed by Raphael : THE COMPANY WE KEEP. BRITAIN'S SHAME IN AFRICA.

While this inquisition was in progress, other media experts rushed to South Africa to do their bit for Britain's conscience.

David Taylor of the BBC found himself and his cameraman mostly crowding into temporary lavatories and unsavoury sleeping quarters, while ignoring the modern and the clean. Commented Lord Kearton of Courtauld's : 'This programme has a definite lavatory obsession.' Such was the standard of reporting. Meanwhile, in South Africa the debate, which started some years before Raphael hit upon the idea, continued in all earnest on issues like PDL (Poverty Datum Line), MSL (the Minimum Subsistence Level), EML (the Effective Minimum Level) and HSL (the Humane Standard of Living). The sensational lavatory approach made the headlines, the latter internal debate brought steady increases in Black wages.

At a Chatham House speech in London Mr Harry Oppenheimer of Anglo-American pointed out that because of this debate in South Africa changes were taking place in any event—without interference from Britain. He hinted rather subtly at the fact that the concern shown by Raphael and his rabble-rousers for Black employees of British firms in South Africa 'is not felt in anything like the same degree in regard to British firms operating, say, in Hong Kong or India, or elsewhere on the African continent'.

Another critic[5] put it rather more bluntly : 'Mr Raphael and his friends tackled the dust on the furniture in South Africa while ignoring the grime on the floors elsewhere where Britain had business interests. On sugar plantations in South Africa Black workers were earning five times the wages paid to tea-leaf pickers in Sri Lanka—the island which used to be known as Ceylon. In the *Daily Mirror* on 2 October 1973 Dr S. Vijeratnam described working conditions on tea plantations in Sri Lanka as follows : 'It is worse than a prison camp. Their quarters aren't fit for animals, let alone human beings.

'In Hong Kong—a British crown colony—lives Yuk-Lan Wong, aged ten. Before and after school she helps her aunt to make key-chain links for a total of twelve to twenty pennies a day.

5. This critic, Judge Gerald Sparrow, who placed an advertisement to this effect in the Fleet Street press, was dismissed together with his organization—the Club of Ten—as a front of the South African Government. After Joan Lestor—Labour's Junior Minister of Foreign Affairs and a leading light in the Anti-Apartheid Movement—investigated, Mr Sparrow and his group were exonerated.

Yuk-Lan is one of more than thirty thousand child labourers in Hong Kong where such exploitation is supposed to be illegal.' Chinese workers doing the same job as Europeans are normally paid only one seventieth to one hundredth of the European wages—by British companies.

The South African monthly wage is higher than in any other African country and the gap between wages paid for Blacks and Whites is substantially narrower than that of Zambia, a Black African state. In the *Sunday Telegraph* during May 1973—one of the few papers to look outside South Africa for wage discrepancies—it was reported that unskilled Black workers earned between £25.40 and £44 per month in South Africa, while in Kenya wages for the unskilled varied between £4 and £14.50 a month. A semi-skilled Black worker in South Africa earns between £30.80 and £55.40 per month, while in Uganda salaries varied between £12 and £24.50. A skilled Black worker in South Africa is paid between £37.50 and £92.40 a month, while in Liberia he earns between £21 and £63 a month. And in South Africa the Black workers usually receive free food, clothing, housing and medical care—a bonus rarely enjoyed elsewhere in Africa.

While reams of copy, dozens of editorials—some of them running to almost thirty inches—were devoted in Fleet Street to the conditions of the Black worker in South Africa, these other areas where Britain had business interests and paid much lower wages remained almost hidden from public view. While the Rodgers Commission spent hundreds of man-hours probing United Kingdom operations in South Africa, some firms in Hong Kong, Sri Lanka and India and a host of other African countries were exploiting workers—both adult and minor—with impunity.

Intent as they were on formulating their disgust and abhorrence for South Africa to satisfy Raphael and his devoted followers in anti-apartheid lane, these British parliamentarians could hardly afford distraction by unimportant details concerning far-off places like Hong Kong and Sri Lanka—and the steaming jungles of darkest Africa. Early in 1974 this Royal Commission under the chairmanship of William Rodgers, MP, issued 'guidelines' for British businesses in South Africa. The few who went to the trouble of finding out that Britain was paying Jamaicans and Indians—and other Coloured workers—in its merchant navy wages well below the Plimsoll line set for Whites, found this instruction booklet rather ironic.

Next to appear on the South African wage scene was a delegation of the British Trade Union Congress led by Vic Feather. In December 1973, shortly after their trip to South Africa, Feather and company issued their own guideline report. Commented the South African opposition daily, the *Rand Daily Mail* : 'South Africans will hardly miss the irony. There is Britain facing its worse economic crisis since the 1930s depression, and being brought to the brink of disaster by the unions. There are strikes, threats of strikes and near-strikes by train drivers, power station engineers, ambulance men and coal miners.

'. . . Trapped between the hammer of our sanctions and the anvil of obdurate unions, Mr Heath (British Prime Minister) has taken sweeping economic steps, including the introduction of a three-day week, to avert collapse. . . . At this moment then, the British Trade Union Congress produces its report on the October visit to South Africa of the TUC delegation. And the main proposal, according to first accounts, turns out to be that the TUC should be permitted to introduce its own brand of labour "know how" to the South African scene.' In effect, then, Feather and his men were offering to export Britain's labour unrest and economic near-collapse—precipitated, according to Mr Heath, by Communists—to South Africa !

But guidebooks for South African employers were not issued only in London. From Washington DC came a booklet issued by the US Department of State. It was aimed at American businesses operating in South Africa. Out there, these moguls were told, Black workers should receive a minimum wage of 140 dollars a month. Someone took the trouble to go to Washington's Census Bureau to determine how many Americans were earning wages below that level. Back came the answer : Twenty-four million—mostly Black. Charity, someone once said, begins at home. In effect the US State Department were expecting higher wage standards than its own in South Africa, a country with a much lower cost of living than that of the United States.

The wage series on South Africa earned Adam Raphael a press award—Investigative Reporter of the Year—and yet another round of television appearances. Simon Brebble of the

BBC was one of those who invited the young star reporter over to 'tell us a little of how he first uncovered the story'. As a good award winner should, Raphael appeared to be quite modest. Accolades for 'those who helped', while claiming credit for starting it all—in a pleasant sort of way. In Denmark, Germany and several other countries the International Anti-Apartheid Movement was already building up pressures in the same field.

Gordon Tether of the *Financial Times* was one of the few in Fleet Street who refused to be taken in by it all : 'The plight of the underprivileged in South Africa has attracted as much attention as it has primarily because of the considerable interest there is in Britain in making things hot for apartheid', he wrote. 'As it is, when it is a matter of mobilizing support for the global attack on world poverty, many of the voices that have been so much to the fore in the South African wages controversy are muted if not entirely silent.'

Adam Raphael did not invent the double-standard in journalism. He was not the first journalist who applied it to South Africa, just as the British Trade Union Congress, the Rodgers Commission and the US Department of State are not the first or only ones in their respective fields. Double-standard journalism has been a regular and prominent feature of the world's approach to South Africa. As Raphael's editor explained afterwards : the *Guardian* was specifically interested in Black wages in South Africa because it wanted to get at her policy of apartheid. Starvation wages elsewhere in the world—even if paid by British business—did not really concern this newspaper.

On 8 June 1971 the *New York Times* urged the US House of Representatives to deny South Africa a share of America's sugar market under the so-called quota system. On 10 June it reiterated its support for an embargo against this country because doing business with South Africa could be interpreted as a 'gift to the practitioners of apartheid'—and was therefore most undesirable. On the very next day it lauded Nixon for 'the ending of legal barriers which have prevented any significant Sino-American trade since the Truman administration'. Said the *Times* : The United States should 'open the way for a massive infusion of American capital and technological expertise' into Red China. Asked some : What does Red China have that South Africa does not possess? An internal policy with which America can identify itself? An external posture that makes it more acceptable? (At that time an American academic calculated the death toll since Mao took over the reins in China as close to twenty-four million.)

And when it comes to any form of tribal self-rule in South Africa—the principle on which apartheid is built—the *New York Times* finds itself groping for adjectives strong enough to express its displeasure. Yet, in discussing the plight of the American Indian on 2 March 1973, the *Times* concluded : 'The Administration can do a lot to ease the present strain if it will carry out President Nixon's own recommendation for greater tribal self-government.' What seems to be excellent sauce for the goose does not apply to the gander. In far-off Australia the same transparent double-standard typifies discussions in the press of policies geared towards tribal self-government in South Africa as opposed to local self-rule for the Aborigine. In the first instance it is decidedly bad—in the latter a praiseworthy move towards healthy self-help among the Aborigines.

In September 1964 Lloyd Garrison of the *New York Times* reported that 70,000 lost their lives in civil strife in Cameroon. His report was given much less prominence than a despatch on the execution of two Black men in South Africa who were found guilty of murdering a court witness. It took the world several months to catch up on the mass-scale killings in Sudan where the annual death toll was estimated at 100,000. When the press started to run the story it received only obscure inside page treatment. Burundi, Uganda and Nigeria hardly managed to stir the press pundits of the world half as much as the fatal shooting of sixty-nine Black demonstrators at Sharpeville in South Africa—although their total death toll topped a million.

On Tuesday night, 12 September 1974, the media's double-standard or selective indignation was once again vividly illustrated when shootings occurred at Carltonville gold mine in South Africa. Black mine workers, after a drinking spree, went on the rampage. In a community of 8,500 mineworkers, hundreds were running around, breaking into stores and attacking officials with axes and pick handles. The mining authorities lost control and called the police to restore the peace. After trying without success to reason with the rioting crowds or to stop them with tear gas and a baton charge the police opened fire. Eleven Black miners were killed. The cause of the unrest was purely economic—one group of Black mineworkers being unhappy about pay increases for another group of their own race.

The overseas press reacted swiftly and somewhat hysterically. A new term quickly found its way into the front-page news columns in London and New York's daily press—'mini-Sharpeville'. The Anti-Apartheid Movement picketed the South African Embassy in London and the British Trade Union Congress insisted on an immediate judicial inquiry. From the United Nations came demands that the world body be allowed to supervise the investigation. Editorial indignation expressed in the overseas press was supplemented with lengthy in-depth analyses—critical and one-sided.

The *Guardian* could hardly contain itself. It saw in this apolitical event the demise of apartheid and the South African 'regime' and it editorialized as follows under the heading STORM SIGNS IN S. AFRICA: 'Events like this are not planned beforehand, any more than the point of a lightning discharge can be predicted with accuracy. But the signs of a forthcoming storm are unmistakable and South Africa has been ready for one all year. This will not necessarily be the last.'

At the same time the killing of more than forty citizens in India's Gujerat region passed almost unnoticed. They were shot by the police while trying to loot grain storage depots. The fact of the matter was that these rioters were starving to death and their act was one of desperation. On 3 January 1974 the *Guardian* was spurred into action. It published a one-inch report on the death of another six rioters in India. Stuck away on the inside pages, the one sentence report simply: 'RIOTERS SHOT. Police shot dead at least six rioters, and the Prime Minister, Mrs Indira Ghandhi, was forced to abandon a public meeting after being pelted with shoes during a 24-hour general strike in the western Indian state of Maharashtra.'

Referring to Burundi, Uganda, Nigeria and the Central African Republic, Dennis Duggan of the American newspaper, *Newsday*, said: 'It is . . . perplexing to ponder the almost total lack of criticism from the world press on such atrocities. Apparently it is simply that Black racists are less offensive to liberals than White racists are.' Wrote *National Review*'s William F. Buckley in his syndicated column during a visit to Africa in early

1974 : 'Duggan is of course correct, and there is in this judgement that sad strain of residual cultural racism which some (e.g. I) find much more offensive than White African Jim Crow. It is the shoulder shrug : when Black people kill Black people, they are doing what comes naturally. When White people discriminate against Black people, they are to be despised.'

Now living in exile in Tanzania, Milton Obote was President of Uganda until he was deposed by Idi Amin, who gained a certain measure of fame or notoriety when he expelled 40,000 Asians. Witnessing subsequent atrocities in Uganda from across the border, Milton Obote wrote : 'Africa would be guilty of double-standards and hypocrisy if it continually condemns oppressive measures in the White-ruled South African states while keeping silent about oppression and genocide in Uganda.' Africa is guilty of hypocrisy and so are large sections of the world press.

Prepare for a violent death. This has been the world media's sordid prognosis for South Africa ever since the Nationalists came to power in 1948. The London *News Chronicle* was one of those which started with regular death notices as early as 1948. Only months after Malan's victory at the polls the *Chronicle* was using words like 'decay' and 'twilight' to describe South Africa's state of health. In 1954 it warned that 'there is only one possible end . . . blood and darkness'. In 1958 the *Chronicle* predicted : 'One day there will be a "Hungarian explosion". And there will be no Red Army to come to the rescue of the oppressors.'

Today there is no *Chronicle* left to further deliberate on South Africa's 'imminent' violent death. The newspaper passed away. And South Africa? In 1973 it appeared ninth among the world's developed nations on the widely acclaimed Business Environment Index (BERI). Prepared at the University of Delaware in the United States, this index is based on criteria such as political stability and economic growth. Britain was one of the many nations outranked by South Africa on this world barometer of stability.

Remarked the Chief Editor of the London *Economist* in the March 1970 issue of *Harper's* magazine : 'The progressives who still believe in predictions of violence in South Africa live in a dreamworld.' Undeterred by BERI or the Editor of the *Econo-*

*mist*, however, they still strut around on stage like Shakespearian soothsayers shouting 'Beware the Ides of March' whenever South Africa is mentioned. A world press stubbornly refusing to give up hope—harping back to that unfortunate day in March 1960 when sixty-nine Blacks were shot and it seemed as if the horsemen of the apocalypse had indeed descended on South Africa.

Obviously dismayed by its own composite of half-truths, negative observations and outright lies masquerading in editorial form under the heading TRUTH ABOUT SOUTH AFRICA, the *Toronto Globe and Mail* concluded in May 1963 that 'South Africa is staggering toward a bloodbath'. This doom prophet approach to South African affairs is still fashionable in Canada and elsewhere. Respected dailies like the *Guardian* and *The Times* in London and the *New York Times* and *Washington Post* have basically the same approach—awed by their phantasmagoric visions of South Africa they naturally conclude that this country is destined to go up in flames.

The extent to which the overseas press frightens its readers with this grotesque version of South Africa was candidly illustrated in March 1973. This was the month in which American Negro John Little first visited this far-off country to attend an evangelical conference. A well-educated and sophisticated citizen from Seattle, Little confided to the South African press that he was scared to death when he heard that he had to travel to South Africa for this conference. A religious man, Little prayed for guidance and protection. Once in Durban, South Africa, he could hardly believe his unhindered existence in a city friendly to him despite his Blackness. Said Mr Little: 'I gained these horrible impressions from reading our newspapers in America.'

Even if Mr Little turned to tourist guides or magazines for factual information on the facilities and scenery of the country he intended visiting, he may have struck on one of many with unadulterated political bias. Whereas the tourist trade hardly finds it difficult to extol the scenic wonders and culinary qualities of Russia or Yugoslavia or Poland without getting involved in political dialectics, it often finds it impossible to afford such luxuries when it comes to South Africa. Wrote 'travel writer' Jacobs in *Africa A to Z*: 'Is this a country to visit? The answer can only be a personal one. Actually to see an immoral authoritarian state—and South Africa is such a state—is to learn for oneself, to benefit from knowledge that can come only from firsthand experience. Some visitors may, of course, wish they had never gone.'[6]

In 1969 *Holiday* magazine in the United States featured as a cover story BEAUTIFUL COUNTRIES—UNPOPULAR GOVERNMENTS. SHOULD YOU VISIT PERU, HAITI, SOUTH AFRICA, EGYPT? the magazine asked. 'South Africa's repression of its Black population horrifies most of the civilized world . . . ' So starts the 'travel' section devoted to this country. Richard Atcheson, who went there to report for *Holiday*, became an instant expert on politics. 'South Africa is a lonely country, full of lonely people', contended Atcheson. 'They are sad, and they are in desperate trouble . . . ' The ruling Nationalists Party 'is schizoid'. Atcheson turned out to be the only happy one—returning to the United States in time to witness a new spate of riots and Black/White killings. It is not explained how South Africa as a democracy happened to be grouped together with three dictatorships.

How does South Africa fare on videotape and celluloid? Not much better than in print. Much worse, some would contend. Oversimplification of a complicated world is one of the outstanding characteristics of television—and advocacy reporting. With 50,000 feet of film on an average to cut to a mere 2,500 feet, it is easy for any man with a mission to make his viewpoint prevail, regardless of the merits of the case.

In the early sixties Fred Friendly of the giant CBS TV network set out to produce 'a special' on South Africa. This American wrote to the South African authorities promising an unbiased and objective review of current affairs—they all do— and was given special facilities. The end product was neither friendly nor objective. Its title, *Sabotage in South Africa*, some suggested, might well have been *Sabotage of South Africa*. This film, scratches streaking across its tired panchro surface, is still

6. In 1964 *The Christian Science Monitor* published a political atlas of Africa indicating only one true democracy, South Africa. The position has not changed much since, yet Jacobs did not advise his readers to study authoritarian states—or genocide—in other parts of Africa first hand. He simply mused over nature's beauty and the friendliness of the natives in darkest Africa.

doing the rounds at anti-South African socials in the United States and until recently served as a primer for State Department trainees in Washington.

In the many years since, CBS and the other big ones in America—ABC, NBC and PBS—have been consistent in their anti-bias whenever anything remotely political and South African came their way. The only objectivity they managed was in programmes on African wild life, diamonds and heart transplants. Not every anti-South African programme screened on American television is an original creation. Often productions on the 'excesses' of 'fascist' South Africa are purchased in Britain. And sometimes these imports are tailored to suit the American market. For example, when *Gold Run*, produced by Briton Anthony Thomas, came into the hands of CBS, the term 'migrant worker' in the British text became 'voluntary slavery' in the American commentary.

Britannia has always ruled the airwaves when it came to TV specials or current affairs programmes about South Africa. Since 1968 British television has accounted for most of the major TV productions about South Africa. During the first six months of 1970 no less than nine documentaries were screened on television channels. With rare exceptions these specials are usually sensational distortions circulating world-wide after their London premières. The titles tell their own story: *The Colour Line*; *Whiter Than Thou*; *The Dumping Grounds*; *South Africa Loves Jesus*; *Last Grave at Dimbaza* and *The Good Ladies of Johannesburg*.

Two competing British producers—John Morgan of Thames–TV and Hugh Burnett of BBC–TV—both called their productions *The Afrikaner*. This was hardly a coincidence. Many of Britain's 'documentaries' about South Africa deal essentially with the Afrikaner in a most uncomplimentary fashion. Morgan subtitled his celluloid treatise on the Afrikaner, *Where Sport and Politics Go Hand-in-hand*. In what was ostensibly a programme on sport in South Africa, filmed during the 1968 British rugby tour, John Morgan portrayed the Afrikaner sportsman as a dour brute bent on avenging the Anglo-Boer War by bashing his British opponents into bloody submission.

By carefully juggling unrelated snippets of recorded interviews and pointing out that the captain of the Springbok rugby team, Dawie de Villiers, also happens to be a religious minister, Morgan contended that sport, politics and religion were all rolled into one in South Africa. Viewing the programme convinced the London *Daily Mirror*'s Mary Malone that those 'Dutch farmers' in far-off South Africa had faith in 'God and the referee' to ensure victory. 'God works best in bodies, made harder and fitter, it seems; and these dour church-going dogged Dutch were sold with the will to win, and a sense of mission that to win is their task.'

Many Britons deplored this travesty of truth. Claude Lister, British-born manager of the South African tennis team, admitted : 'It made my blood boil.' Famous Welsh rugby player Cliff Morgan, after receiving several letters of protest, made haste to explain in public that he had nothing to do with the programme and was not even distantly related to John Morgan. Cliff Morgan did accompany the British rugby team on its tour of South Africa and saw it all. 'It looked to me as if they were trying to take the mickey out of the Afrikaner,' he said. 'It wasn't my report, and what appeared was not what I saw.'

In his fifty-minute essay, *The Afrikaner*, in 1970, Hugh Burnett of the BBC pictured this 'White tribe that rules South Africa' as isolationist Bible-pounders on the defence. 'Authoritative' spokesmen included men like Gert Yssel proselytizing against the evils of the mini-skirt—obscure men who stood ridiculed by their own people. With careful selection of such Afrikaner 'mouthpieces' and ingenious editing Burnett could afford to restrict his own comment to a bare minimum. A measure of the lasting success of the programme is the fact that television in Zambia still gave the programme prime time treatment three years later.

Bashfulness has never plagued British television. In April 1970 Granada Television announced that it would not present any of the games played by the visiting South African cricket team as a sporting event as this would imply acceptance of the 'unsporting principles that were the basis for the selection of the team'. Several newspapers questioned this boycott. The London *Sun* aptly described it as 'political censorship of sports news'. While this storm was still brewing, Granada approached South African officialdom in the London Embassy requesting a sporting chance to film apartheid in action in South Africa. Said programme director Geoff Moore in a letter addressed to the Ambassador : 'We would like to take an objective, balanced look at the progress of the homelands policy.'

South Africa being 'a dictatorship', Granada's team had no problem to obtain ingress despite its ban on South African cricket games in Britain. The end result was neither cricket nor sporting. Entitled, *The Dumping Grounds*, this Granada special did not focus on the homelands at all, but on a so-called resettlement area some two hundred miles from Johannesburg. Briefed by a local anti-government crusader, Father Cosmos Desmond, Granada set out to record in sight and sound isolated cases of marasmas, palarga, kwashiorkor, and malnutrition at Schmidtsdrift. Nobody who saw the programme would have suspected that South Africa was the undisputed leader in Africa as far as nutrition, medical services, housing and a host of other facilities for its Black denizens were concerned.

Bishop Wheeldon protested strongly as Chairman of the governing body of St Michael's Mission Hospital, which featured in the programme. The Mission Hospital, said Wheeldon, 'deplores the use, for publicity purposes, of totally fictitious figures ostensibly relating to conditions at this hospital'. He found much of the material shown 'out of character with the work being done in the area by the South African authorities and the staff of the hospital'. At the United Nations, where the Anti-Apartheid Committee arranged special showings, there was unreserved praise. Prominent on the opening night was a sea of Black faces representing parts of Africa where starvation already assumed catastrophic dimensions. These were Black UN Ambassadors revelling at the blow this film struck on behalf of their campaign against White-ruled South Africa.

It took *Time* and *Newsweek* another four years to stumble on the real crisis areas of Africa. In some cases it was obvious why it took them so long. Reported *Newsweek*'s Jaffe in August 1974 : 'The pride—or terror—of [Black African] governments kept them from admitting the scope of the problem or sounding a timely alarm. . . . This was particularly true in Ethiopia, where local officials long ago reported to the Cabinet that a northern famine had begun. When frantic men, women and children fleeing drought-stricken Wollo province appeared near Addis Ababa, authorities locked them up and left them to starve.' In others where helpless thousands starved to death out in the open, the media only had their myopia to blame.

Wrote Jaffe in *Newsweek*: 'In camps across north-central Africa, 1.5 million men, women and children are leading a brink-of-death existence. They are refugees from the great drought that has scourged sixteen African nations for several years. At best the camps provide the barest food and health care; at worst, they are hellholes. But the Africans who inhabit the camps are, in a way, the lucky ones. Another million Africans have already died of hunger and disease. Five to ten million more are starving in the African bush or the slums of drought-area towns.'

In the Sahel, reported *Time* during May 1974, mass starvation is an immediate problem. Including Chad, Mali, Mauritania, Niger, Senegal and Upper Volta, Sahel's flat savannas are now empty 'save for the thousands of reddish brown mounds that mark the graves of those who starved'. Shantytown refugee camps have risen like festering sores throughout the region, providing the barest relief to half a million people. In Chad, said *Time*, some emaciated nomads begged a UN official not to send them medicines, pleading that death from diphtheria was quicker and hence easier than the slower death from starvation.

Television in Britain—and elsewhere—has yet to take a serious look at starving Black Africa. Preoccupied with a few isolated hospitalized cases of malnutrition in South Africa, they are impervious to the plight of the dying masses to the north. Some may have noticed and decided that it was simply not sound politics to point the camera lens to festering sores in Black Utopia, while 'wicked' South Africa was still around.

In 1970 it became clear also that even the most rudimentary technical standards of television in Britain, the United States and elsewhere can be waived as long as the intent is decidedly anti-South African. *End of a Dialogue* has a certain home-movie quality that immediately tells even the most unenlightened that it was not produced by professionals. This *cinema verité* style may even have commended it to the BBC when the film was introduced by Nana Mahomo. A self-styled 'freedom fighter', representing one faction of the exiled militant Pan-African Congress in London, Mahomo claimed that it was secretly shot by members of the PAC in South Africa and smuggled to Britain.

The other faction of the PAC disowned the film. *End of a*

*Dialogue*, they said, was not made by the Black organization but by White liberals who then labelled it as a PAC production, presumably to increase its commercial value. 'Anyone could have made the film', they said. 'All the drama about them risking their liberty is absolute nonsense. Photographs such as those seen in the film are displayed daily in the South African press.' But the BBC was not to be discouraged by a dissident faction of the PAC. In presenting *End of a Dialogue* on prime time in November 1970 the BBC's Desmond Wilcox claimed that those who made the film 'risked both their lives and liberty'. The filming equipment, he contended, was smuggled into South Africa by sympathetic White visitors because if any Black South African purchased professional cameras in the Republic the authorities would immediately become suspicious!

Those who expected a keyhole view of the secret world of apartheid must have been disappointed by the uneven camera trip through everyday South Africa's good and bad spots. The scene selection was obviously geared to portraying Blacks only in poverty and Whites in affluence—almost like Harlem and Scarsdale, New York, in juxtaposition as a portrayal of life in the United States. The meat was in the commentary in the shape of dubious statistics. As the film ended, compère Wilcox reappeared. The South African Ambassador, he said, was invited to discuss the film on TV with producer Nana Mahomo and Abdul Minty, Secretary of the Anti-Apartheid Movement. He declined.

Having the South African Ambassador, Nana Mahomo and Abdul Minty on the same programme would, of course, have been tantamount to joining together in open discussion an American Ambassador, Angela Davis and Stokely Carmichael— or having a British Ambassador in public debate with leaders of the Irish Republican Army. Desmond Wilcox nevertheless insisted that his invitation to South Africa's chief representative in Britain was a reasonable one—and he saw little merit in South Africa's insistence that it be given equal opportunity to show a film of its own choice on BBC television.

South African Ambassador Luttig instead wrote to BBC Chairman Lord Hill, pointing out eleven flagrant lies in *End of a Dialogue*. For instance, Mahomo claimed that 50 per cent of all the Black children in South Africa died before the age of five—the real figure happened to be 10 per cent, which is much lower than elsewhere in Africa; it was charged that the life expectancy of Blacks in South Africa was 34, while in fact UN publications put it at 46—one of the highest in the continent; kwashiorkor and trachoma, it was alleged, took a heavy toll among Blacks in South Africa, while the incidence of the first is only 0.7 per cent and the latter 0.35 per cent; Mahomo said that there was no sanitation in Soweto, largest of the Black urban areas—and water had to be carried some distance, while, in fact, this township enjoys all the essential services such as electricity, water, roads, transport and waterborne sewerage.

When the South African Ambassador failed to accept his invitation, Wilcox invited two Conservative parliamentarians, Harold Soref and Patrick Wall, to the studio to speak up for the 'other side'. In doing so he mounted a tiger. Leading the contra-viewpoint Soref described *End of a Dialogue* as 'worthy of the late Dr Joseph Goebbels'. He added: 'I believe it was psychological warfare against the White man which the BBC have exposed and it was part of a campaign that the BBC exercises against any country that is fighting Communism, whether it is Greece, Vietnam, Rhodesia, Portugal or South Africa. I feel that you could produce a film equally slanted about Britain. . . .' Wilcox hastily requested Mr Soref to confine his observations to general points and all the while the Conservative politician became increasingly specific—touching not only on this one programme but several others where the BBC showed a leftist bias.

Referring briefly to another film presented on BBC by the well-known South African Communist, Ruth First, Harold Soref proceeded to relate how another Conservative MP, John Biggs-Davison's invitation had been withdrawn by the BBC and he had been replaced by Basil Davidson on a panel discussion of the Guinea situation. Mr Biggs-Davison was informed that the BBC had to cancel his appearance 'owing to pressure'. It so happened that he had been in Guinea frequently and was sympathetic to the Portuguese, while Mr Davidson was a severe critic of the authorities.

*End of a Dialogue* has since been screened on television in the United States, the Netherlands, Sweden, New Zealand and a host of other countries. Technical excellence is hardly a prerequisite for success when it comes to television—it's bias that counts. But what about film festivals? In 1971 this production made its appearance at the Oberhausen Short Film Festival as one of two films entered by the British Foreign Office Panel for Film Festivals! *End of a Dialogue* won three awards.

In 1974 the anti-South African forces in London offered the BBC another 'clandestine production', *Last Grave at Dimbaza.* Stated a report in the London *Times*: 'One of the Englishmen, the film-maker cum soundman, came from television and had been instrumental in smuggling out *End of a Dialogue*; the other, the cameraman, was fresh out of film school. . . . Getting into South Africa was easy, their new 16 mm camera could fit into a shoulder bag and, in a country devoted to home movies, looked suitably amateur; their tape recorder, of a type developed for the CIA, was the size of a cigarette packet.'

It had all the elements of suspense and drama—and the film was 'suitably amateur' to make the grade on television and in film festivals. The focal point is Dimbaza, a Black township in the Ciskei homeland of South Africa. Described by the viciously anti-Government South African Institute of Race Relations as 'neat', Dimbaza is none the less pictured by these 'underground' film-makers as a death trap for Blacks. In answering the charges made in this film, the South African Embassy, among other things, pointed out that the death rate at Dimbaza was 'actually lower than that recorded for a number of boroughs in the United Kingdom'.

At about the same time two Swedish television men, Per Sanden and Rudi Spee, released their shock treatise on 'the massacre of Caprivi'—a finger-shaped extension of South African administrated South-West Africa. Relying on the tales of one Black man and parading a series of unidentified human skulls, the Swedes proclaimed with horror that no fewer than 105 defenceless Blacks were massacred by South African troops in 1968. Reacting to a strong challenge from South Africa and contradictory facts, the producers first changed the 'death toll' to sixty-three, then decided that 'perhaps' there may have been two massacres instead of one!

In the meantime the South African authorities facilitated a first-hand investigation of Caprivi by the world press. The Swedes, although formally invited, were not among the thirty-two who toured Caprivi in search of evidence. Introducing the Sanden creation on Swedish television shortly afterwards, Magnus Flaxen dismissed the evidence of the thirty-two newsmen that there were no signs of a massacre, as 'predictable' and 'hardly objective'. Facts have never prevented South Africa's enemies on world television from getting their viewpoint across.

In early 1972 Merrill Panitt, Editor of America's mass circulation *TV Guide*, painted the picture of the United States projected on European television screens as follows : 'It is seen as imperialistic and warlike, bent on dominating Southeast Asia and the emerging countries of Africa, which it is preparing to exploit. . . . It is described as a place where Blacks live in near-slavery . . . it is alleged to be plagued with poverty because capitalists want it that way. . . . It is pictured as forcing millions of young people, concerned about Vietnam, crime and pollution, to turn to hard drugs. . . . It is projected as a corrupt, dangerous place where walking on the streets—anywhere and everywhere—is an invitation to be robbed and/or murdered.'

The impact of all this on viewers is so strong, contended Panitt, so pervasive, that even loyal Americans working abroad confess that each time they are scheduled to go home on leave they experience real fear about what they will find there. This liberal editor had no hesitation in ascribing much of what happens to the American image on British, Dutch, Swedish and other European networks to leftist bias in the medium. Explains Panitt : ' "Left" can mean anything from a middle-of-the-road member of the Socialist Party to Communist, Maoist or anarchist.'

To the Leagues of the Left who so effectively control the electronic media in Europe and the United States, every country which could be vaguely classified as 'Right' serves as a target. Hence television's deep concern about 'oppression' in America, while heaping unreserved praise on mainland China where the road to greatness happened to be paved with some twenty million corpses; thus world television's obvious lack of interest in the starvation of thousands in the Third World, while lashing out at the White authorities for 'allowing' isolated cases of kwashior-kor and trachoma to occur among rural Blacks in South Africa.

On 6 April 1970 the London *Daily Telegraph* depicted the bias at the BBC where most of the vitriol against South Africa is brewed for export : 'Most BBC producers probably do make an effort to be impartial', said the *Telegraph*. 'But, whether due to natural inclination or defective education, their political centre is in many cases so far to the Left as to render their efforts laughable. Their genuine idea of a balanced discussion is between Left and Far-Left—Bernstein vs Marx, Crosland vs. Marcuse, Jack Straw vs. Cohn-Bendit, Palme vs. Palme-Dutt, Kenneth Tynan vs. Dr Leary. The Right for them is an unknown land, filled with malign monsters and mirages.'

Said Abdul Minty, Secretary of the Anti-Apartheid Movement, at the United Nations in 1971 : 'All channels of the BBC have produced very useful films recently. The film-makers approach us and consult us and we give them ideas for subjects and also how to go about filming them.' These films, he explained, had to be increasingly shocking, because the public might soon get bored with the whole subject. And so the BBC helps actively in the assault on White South Africa. . . .

As elsewhere in Europe, Panitt of *TV Guide* found British television, 'especially news and public affairs departments, populated by young left-leaning intellectuals, who somehow feel it is their mission to denigrate the American civilization'. Much of what appears on European television, added Panitt regretfully, originates at the four big networks in the United States. It is always the negative on ABC, NBC, CBS and PBS that makes the grade overseas—not the positive. He contended, however, that this should not inhibit honest debate within the United States, regardless of the devastating effect such self-criticism may have abroad.

The debate, it turns out, is not always honest. *The Selling of the Pentagon* was one of CBS's most successful productions on the overseas circuit. In the end it proved to be nothing more than a grossly inaccurate propaganda piece bent on discrediting the 'military establishment'. By, for example, splicing together six completely unrelated utterances of a public address by Colonel MacNeil, CBS made them appear continuous. After an interview with another Pentagon official, Daniel Henkin, CBS rearranged its questions. Henkin was prepared. He kept a tape recorder going during the interview. On another occasion CBS staged a so-called 'pot party' among students in Chicago and used this as evidence of widespread use of drugs among upper-class college youths—despite existing narcotics laws.

In South Africa television is still to be introduced, but there are many who contend that too much of the adverse comment that appears in foreign print originates locally in the English language opposition press. Written in a familiar tongue, the opposition journals are easily understood abroad, while the Afrikaans press in support of the Government is rarely quoted. The consensus remains, however, that it would be a sad day if South Africa found herself forced to stifle honest internal debate and self-criticism for the sake of withholding incriminating material from enemies abroad.

Some episodes obviously strengthen the hands of those who advocate steps against the English-language press. The 'prison controversy' of the mid-sixties was such an episode. It involved the *Rand Daily Mail* in Johannesburg, its editor Laurence Gandar and reporter Benjamin Pogrund. Released to the world mass media shortly before the opening of the UN Congress on the Prevention of Crime and Treatment of offenders in Stockholm, the *Rand Daily Mail's* jail series were based on the un-corroborated testimony of ex-political prisoner Harold Strachan —as told to Pogrund.

On his arrival in Southampton *en route* to the Swedish capital, the South African Commissioner of Prisons was confronted by a contingent of newsmen armed with copies of the article. His efforts to discredit these sweeping allegations of brutality and torture met with cynical comment. In Stockholm an army of abusive placard-bearers awaited him. Meanwhile in South Africa even some English-language opposition dailies were disturbed by this turn of events.

Said the *Natal Sunday Tribune* : 'Allegations, if they are to stick, must first be proved. This has yet to be done. But already the professional castigators overseas have gloried in a heaven-sent opportunity to wield the big stick against South Africa once more. For them, allegations become facts overnight.'

Retorted Gandar : 'We are just doing a straight newspaper job and it is not our fault if this is misrepresented or exploited.' Congratulations came from Moscow, Peking, Cairo, Accra, London and New York, among others. Moscow radio lauded the *Rand Daily Mail* for 'exposing once more the terrible regime reigning in Verwoerd's prisons'.

A series of court cases followed in South Africa. Strachan was proven an outright liar. Found guilty on one count of perjury and two counts under the Prison Act, which makes it an offence to publicise untruths about prison conditions, he went back to jail where he spent some time before conviction as an explosives expert and saboteur. 'Strachan,' noted magistrate M. E. Goodhead, 'skilfully used harmless facts on which to build his edifice of lies—the lies, which as this case has shown, it has been difficult, laborious and obviously a costly matter for the State to disprove. Strachan was only too keen that his lies should receive wide publicity.'

The jail series earned Gandar and Pogrund a conviction and fine in South Africa—and abroad for the *Rand Daily Mail* the 1966 World Press Achievement Award of the American Newspaper Publishers Association. The *Rand Daily Mail*, said the ANPA, is 'one of the world's leading crusaders' and has 'often been the target of government action'. The ANPA sympathized with Strachan in being 'sentenced to two and a half years in prison for *allegedly* having lied'.

The ANPA considered Gandar and the *Rand Daily Mail* fearless opponents of a gruesome police state machinery in South Africa. Yet the mass circulation opposition *Johannesburg Sunday Times* found it necessary to praise the authorities for their tolerance. 'The South African Government', said the *Times*, 'surprising though it may seem, can also take some credit. People overseas who criticize our Government so readily should now realize that the award to the *Rand Daily Mail* would not be possible if we did not enjoy press freedom in South Africa.'

While South Africa's English-language press rarely indulge in dishonest smear tactics against their own country abroad, 'stringers' often seem to have no scruples in selling their own environment down the drain for money. Explained Edgar Bernstein, himself a stringer : 'Some overseas reports purporting to come from South African correspondents are not honest criticism, and not reports of facts, but slanderous distortions which do the country harm, and do not help solve its complex problems. I have been confronted with this kind of slanderous material by an overseas editor writing to me : "Your story doesn't tally with so-and-so's story published in such and such. We don't want you to soft-pedal the news." '

Stringers like Bernstein who refuse to string along are dismissed as soft-pedallers. They are dispensable. There will always be other mercenaries who are willing to hard-pedal—to speak out loudly, abusively and dishonestly whether it be for money or political gain. Men with the unhappy flair, in the words of Sir Winston Churchill, for blackguarding their homeland outside their homeland.

In this world of advocacy reporting in print and on the air-waves, South African reality has long been buried and forgotten. There is no need for the Big Lie when heavy concentration on the negative to the exclusion of the positive can accomplish the same result. Selective indignation and double-standards will manage to keep South Africa (and a few other select targets) in the searching spotlight while allowing the 'Utopias of the Left' to go about their wrongs in the dark with impunity. And firm Leftist control of the media ensures that South Africans will not easily have cause to lose their penchant for Jefferson's second statement as they observe their own country's treatment in the world press: 'Nothing can now be believed. . . . '

# Index